LIMN NUMBER FIVE

EBOLA'S ECOLOGIES

edited by: **Stephen J. Collier**, **Christopher M. Kelty** and
Andrew Lakoff

I0419287

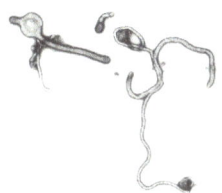

Preface

In the wake of the 2014 Ebola epidemic, global health officials have been widely criticized for a lack of preparedness. But how was preparedness initially constituted as a problem for health authorities, what systems of response were built to address this problem, and how will preparedness be rethought given the failures of response in 2014?

BY **ANDREW LAKOFF, STEPHEN J. COLLIER** AND **CHRISTOPHER M. KELTY**

It was an unprecedented outbreak; it never happened before. There were a lot of things we didn't know at that time. No one could have imagined that it would be what we have now.

—Pierre Rollin, US Centers for Disease Control, December 2014 (quoted in Sack et al 2014)

SUPER-EBOLA (1989)

At the plenary session of the 1989 Annual Meeting of the American Society of Tropical Medicine and Hygiene, Colonel Llewellyn J. Legters, an epidemiologist at the Army Uniformed Services Hospital specializing in tropical disease, led the audience in a scenario-based exercise. The exercise unfolded as follows:

In the spring of 1991, as tensions escalated between rebel factions and the ruling government of the fictional country of Changa, 200,000 refugees fled to neighboring countries where they faced starvation and disease. Hundreds of US Peace Corps volunteers, Christian aid workers, and American military personnel were working in refugee camps to provide medical care and improve hygiene.

In this context, a novel and terrifying disease appeared: at least two-dozen refugees had died of a mysterious ailment, with symptoms that included headaches, vomiting, rash, and gastrointestinal bleeding. Several US members of an international peacekeeping force were stricken with the disease and returned to Fort Bragg. Two of these soldiers then died of liver failure. An army colonel classified the situation as a "global epidemiological emergency." The State Department reported that several civilian volunteers had died after returning to the US on commercial flights, on which they encountered "thousands of people who they might have exposed to the disease." A number of medical volunteers fell ill in the field, and anxiety was growing among civilian health workers.

Specialists became increasingly concerned that the disease was a mutant, easily transmissible strain of Ebola, a disease for which there was no treatment, no vaccine, and no laboratory-based method of diagnosis. If so, health authorities faced an epidemiological nightmare: a disease that combined high virulence, high transmissibility, and the absence of effective treatments. One participant in the exercise, alluding to a famed science fiction scenario from the late 1960s, commented: "You say this might be a strain of Ebola that is respiratorily transmitted. Well, if that is the case it would be very close to Andromeda."

Both relevant experts and necessary equipment were in short supply. A State Department official noted that only four people in the US Public Health Service (PHS) had experience with hemorrhagic fever. Investigators in the field made an urgent request for a portable biocontainment laboratory, but only one was available and it was needed in the US. The State Department searched for pre-packaged field hospitals to send but could not find any that were equipped for contagious disease outbreaks. The foreign quarantine branch of CDC had been, a PHS official explained, "effectively emasculated by budget cuts."

The U.S. military also lacked expertise and equipment to deal with the situation: "We have insufficient expert manpower to sustain appropriate levels of health care, and inadequate supplies," reported an Army General. Nor could international organizations augment American resources: "At all times the infectious disease unit at WHO is running on a shoestring," said an international health official. As the exercise continued, the disease spread unchecked as infected civilian aid workers and military peacekeepers fled the zone and brought the disease back to their home countries.[1]

DIAGNOSING THE PROBLEM

The "Super Ebola" exercise stimulated reflection among the international health experts on the problem of emerging disease, and pointed them toward a diagnosis: we are not prepared. "You never think such a thing could happen, and then it does," commented CDC physician Louisa Campbell. "And you're caught totally unprepared" (Garrett 1990). William Reeves, an expert on insect-borne disease control from UC Berkeley, noted that the lessons of the exercise were not limited to Ebola:

> *"You could take any disease as a model – Ebola, malaria, whatever – and it would reveal the same thing. We aren't ready. Where are the people? The expertise? The equipment? Some planning needs to be done on this" (ibid.).*

In the seminal 1993 volume *Emerging Viruses*, Legters and two colleagues published what they called a "News Report of the Future," which included a fictional Special Report by an interagency working group on the lessons learned from the "Super-Ebola" pandemic. "To put it succinctly," summarized Legters, "the outbreak has con-

firmed, in a very dramatic way, just how ill-prepared we are to detect global epidemic disease threats in a timely fashion, and, once detected, to respond appropriately" (Legters et. al. 1993: 277). This lack of preparedness was especially alarming, he argued, since the world could expect an increasing number of epidemic emergencies due to a number of factors: growth in human population, overcrowded cities, human intrusions into previously uninhabited areas, civil wars leading to crowded refugee camps, and commercial travel that could rapidly spread diseases around the world.

Today, more than two decades later, Legters' diagnosis may seem self-evident and unremarkable. However, it is worth underscoring its novelty at the time. The expectation that international health authorities should be in a state of ongoing preparedness for the emergence of a novel pathogen was just being established in the 1980s. Indeed, exercises like the 1989 Super-Ebola simulation were among the events that helped to establish preparedness as a central problem and norm for global health.

To address the problem of preparedness, Legters proposed the development of a global infrastructure for detecting and managing future outbreaks. Such an infrastructure would include "a surveillance system that can identify unusual disease occurrences near their point of origin; a laboratory system that can quickly characterize the causative agents; a reporting system that alerts the world health community; and a way to institute controls" (Legters, et. al. 1993: 279). Among these elements, Legters focused in particular on the need for a global disease surveillance network, endorsing a proposal made by D.A.

---

1   This description is based on a *Newsday* article by Laurie Garrett (1990). See also Garrett (1994).

Henderson, who had led the WHO smallpox eradication campaign, for epidemiological research centers around the world that could serve as "'listening posts' to identify epidemiological events that might signal global epidemic disease threats" (Legters et. al. 1993: 280).

At this time, in the early 1990s, a range of advocates for the "emerging diseases worldview" (King 2002) proposed similar preparedness measures. And over the next several years, many of these proposals were implemented in some fashion. A global outbreak alert and response network was set up; tools and capacities for the laboratory identification of emerging diseases were built in a number of regional centers; incentives to address the lack of biomedical counter-measures to manage novel disease threats were developed; and a framework for governing global emergency health response was established. In some sense, then, the scenario of a severe Ebola epidemic provided both a motivation and a model for assembling the contemporary infrastructure of "global health security" (Collier and Lakoff 2008).

EBOLA'S ECOLOGIES (2014)

What, then, are we to make of CDC epidemiologist Pierre Rollin's claim—cited in the epigraph to this preface—that "no one could have imagined" the Ebola epidemic of 2014? What, precisely, was unimaginable about the event? As we have seen, it is not that global health authorities had never contemplated an Ebola epidemic of this scale or severity. A much broader epidemic, involving a much more dangerous strain of Ebola, had been explicitly imagined by international health experts twenty-five years earlier. Nor was it the prospect that an Ebola outbreak might prove especially difficult to manage in a conflict or post-conflict situation. Nor, finally, was it the difficulty encountered in mobilizing trained personnel, deploying mobile infectious disease treatment units, or coordinating response through a World Health Organization that had been reduced by budget cuts. Legters and others had anticipated all of this. Indeed, these considerations provided the rationale for early proposals to create a global health preparedness infrastructure.

Rather, it seems, what was surprising to experts like Rollin in 2014 was that "normal" Ebola—and not a strain of "super-Ebola" or some other novel pathogen—could produce such a widespread epidemic given that all prior outbreaks had been limited to small geographical areas and to relatively low numbers of cases (see Lakoff, this issue). According to the 1989 scenario, the catastrophic outcome was a result of the exceptional characteristics of the pathogen itself—its virulence and transmissibility. Given this focus on pathogenicity, setting up an apparatus of preparedness that focused narrowly on disease identification and monitoring seemed to be an adequate response. In 2014, however, it turned out that the severity of the epidemic was due to factors that had not been contemplated by the designers of the "Super-Ebola" exercise—factors that were not addressed by the minimalist infrastructure of global health security that was designed and built in its wake. Among these were: the absence of basic health infrastructure in much of the region, making it difficult to isolate patients and trace contacts; limited capacities of humanitarian NGOs to manage the spread of the disease on their own; and health authorities' inability to enroll a skeptical public in disease prevention efforts and in case reporting.

So what are we to make of this? What can we learn about the contemporary field of global health—and its limits—from the epidemic? The existing infrastructure of global health preparedness, as we have seen, focused narrowly on the rapid detection and containment of a novel pathogen. The events of 2014, by contrast, seem to indicate the need for a more expansive vision of preparedness—one that would break down existing institutional boundaries and divisions of labor: between international health organizations and national governments; between humanitarian medical response, state-based public health, and private sector drug development; and between the routine practices of public health and the acute management of health emergencies.

This issue of *Limn*, on the ecologies of Ebola 2014, examines how the epidemic has put the norms, practices, and institutional logics of contemporary global health into question, and looks at the new assemblages that are being forged in its wake. The concept of "disease ecology" typically refers to a pathogen's relationship to a natural milieu—particularly animal hosts and their environmental niche—and to how this milieu is affected by human behavior. Here, however, we conceive of Ebola's ecologies more broadly to include the administrative, technical, political, and social relationships through which disease outbreaks evolve, and into which experts and officials are now trying to intervene in anticipation of future outbreaks.

Our discussion of the super-Ebola scenario above points to one such ecological relation: that between the pathogen and the apparatus of global health security. From this perspective, the surprising severity of the 2014 outbreak can be explained in part by the limitations of the health preparedness infrastructure that was built as a result of scenarios like the 1989 Super-Ebola pandemic. The current epidemic has also drawn attention to other critical elements of Ebola's changing ecology, including medical humanitarianism, drug development, and risk communication (see the essays by Redfield, Nading, and King, respectively). The contributors to this issue draw on long-term research in these various domains both to understand the "event" of Ebola 2014 and to place it in a broader perspective, addressing questions such as: what has been revealed about the ambitions and the limitations of humanitarian medical response? What are we learning about the assumptions that undergird the contemporary organization of global health security? Are new models of biotechnical innovation being established in the midst of the crisis?

Collectively, the essays suggest a distinctive critical vantage in a field that is saturated with observers. Policy makers, officials, health experts and other critical commentators have rushed to diagnose failure, assign responsibility, and propose ameliorative measures. In contrast, the contributors to "Ebola's Ecologies" take a step back from such assessments to examine how, amid the Ebola 2014 epidemic, the very terrain of global health may be undergoing transformation.

For example, many critics have placed blame for the lack of available medical counter-measures against Ebola on the profit-orientation of the multinational pharmaceutical industry. Closer examination, however, points to a more complicated story about how research and development priorities are established not only in the global drug industry, but also in philanthropic ventures to deal with "neglected" diseases and national biodefense initiatives targeted at "select agents" (see Nading, this volume). Moreover, the emergency has sparked attempts to shape novel platforms of experimentation that can bridge regulatory demands, humanitarian imperatives, and industry expectations (see Kelly, this volume). Meanwhile, some critics have argued that an over-emphasis on pandemic preparedness drew attention away from necessary investment in public health infrastructure in poor countries. But Fearnley counters that this opposition may be overdrawn: the epidemic demonstrates that classical public health and health preparedness are necessarily complementary. Moreover, he argues, the Ebola epidemic shows that preparedness is of vital concern to rich and poor countries alike. These and other contributions to this issue suggest the need to shift our critical gaze: from an exclusive concern with diagnosing failure, to the analysis of how Ebola 2014 has made visible the limitations of existing norms, institutions and practices, as well as the possibilities for a new politics of global health.

BIBLIOGRAPHY

Collier, Stephen J. and Andrew Lakoff. 2008. "The Problem of Securing Health," in Lakoff and Collier, eds., *Biosecurity Interventions: Global Health and Security in Question*. New York: Columbia University Press.

Garrett, Laurie. 1990. "A Medical War Game." *Newsday*. Jan 23rd.

Garrett, Laurie. 1994. *The Coming Plague: Newly Emerging Diseases in a World Out of Balance*. New York: Farrar, Strauss, Giroux.

King, Nicholas. 2002. "Security, Disease, Commerce: Ideologies of Postcolonial Global Health. *Social Studies of Science* 32(5-6):763 – 789.

Legters, Llewellyn J., Linda H. Brink, and Ernest T. Takafuji. 1993. "Are we prepared for a viral epidemic emergency?" in Stephen S. Morse, ed., *Emerging Viruses*. New York: Oxford University Press, pp. 269 – 282

Sack, Kevin, Sheri Fink, Pam Belluck and Adam Nossiter. 2014. "How Ebola Roared Back." *New York Times*, December 29th.

limn is published as needed. This issue is set using Christian Schwartz' Graphik, Dino dos Santos' Leitura and Velino Poster, and Hoefler & Co.'s Whitney typefaces. Layout by **Martin Hoyem/ American Ethnography.** The General Editors of Limn are **Stephen J. Collier, Christopher M. Kelty,** and **Andrew Lakoff.** ‖ This magazine copyright © 2015 the Editors and Martin Hoyem. All articles herein are copyright © 2015 by their respective authors. This magazine may not be reproduced without permission, however the articles are available online at http://limn.it/ and available for unrestricted use under a Creative Commons 3.0 unported License, http://creativecommons.org/ licenses/by-sa/3.0/ ‖ Copyediting provided by Michelle Treviño. ‖ Publication assistance provided by the Research Cluster in Science, Technology and Society at the University of Southern California and the Institute for Society and Genetics at UCLA. More at http:// limn.it/

COVER PHOTO: KERRY TOWN TREATMENT CENTRE IN SIERRA LEONE, 2014 BY: UK MINISTRY OF DEFENCE, THE NATIONAL ARCHIVES; CONTAINS PUBLIC SECTOR INFORMATION LICENSED UNDER THE OPEN GOVERNMENT LICENCE V3.0.

EBOLA 2014

Disease ecology typically focuses on a pathogenic organism's relation to its milieu—in particular, animal hosts and their ecological niche—and on how this milieu is affected by human behavior. But the 2014 Ebola outbreak brings to light the limitations of this notion of ecology. As the articles in this issue make clear, the concept of disease ecology must also include the technical, political and social elements that shape whether an outbreak is rapidly contained or becomes a catastrophic epidemic.

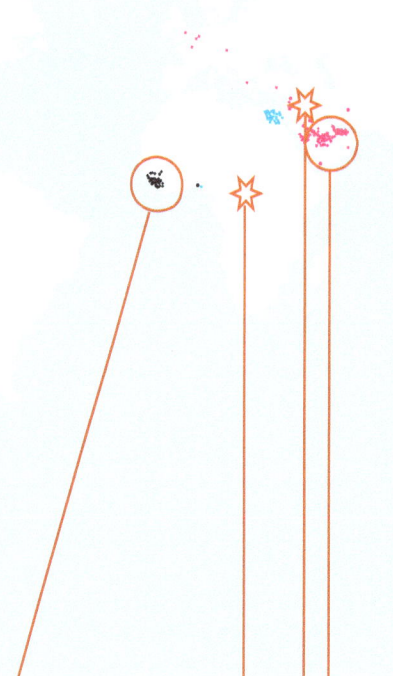

GLOBAL HEALTH SECURITY

Focuses on detecting and containing emerging disease outbreaks so that they do not spread to threaten global economies and populations. During the 2014 Ebola epidemic, there was no intensive global health security response until the disease spread beyond poor West African nations.

HUMANITARIAN BIOMEDICINE

Engages in acute response to neglected diseases in resource poor, typically rural settings. In Spring 2014, it proved incapable of managing a complex and rapidly spreading Ebola outbreak in the absence of local health infrastructure.

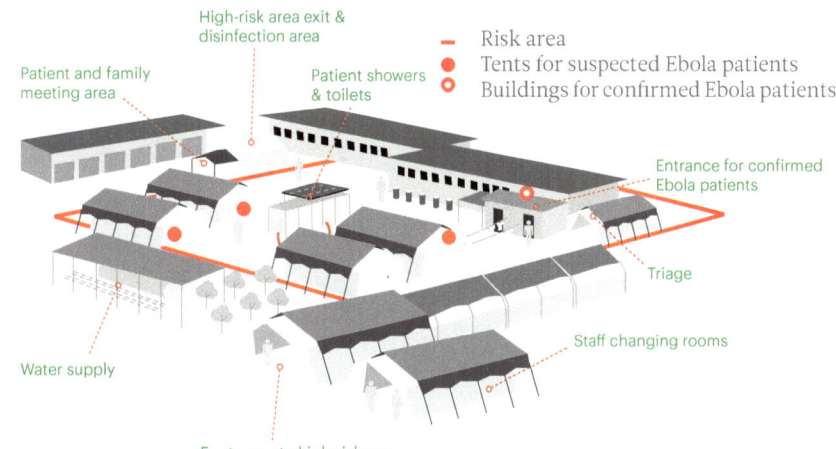

High-risk area exit & disinfection area

Patient and family meeting area

Patient showers & toilets

— Risk area
● Tents for suspected Ebola patients
○ Buildings for confirmed Ebola patients

Entrance for confirmed Ebola patients

Triage

Staff changing rooms

Water supply

Engtrance to high-risk area

CLASSICAL PUBLIC HEALTH

Includes hospital facilities, clinicians, basic supplies, sanitation systems and laboratories. Political crisis, economic reforms and civil conflict left glaring absences in such infrastructure, making it impossible to contain the outbreak in its early stages.

BIOTECHNOLOGY AND DRUG DEVELOPMENT

Targets diseases that have existing markets or other sources of investment such as philanthropies or biodefense. Potential Ebola drugs and vaccines had not been supported through clinical trials in time to make treatment or prevention possible in the early stages of the outbreak.

Outbreak of Unknown Origin in the Tripoint Zone

Guillaume Lachenal traces the urgent past of the current ebola outbreak, offering some surprising lessons about borders.

It was the first time the disease appeared in Sierra Leone. It began to make the news in June. Dozens of British newspapers covered the story over the summer. The *Liverpool Post* started on June 7, announcing an "investigation" from a "Medical Research Council research worker [who] has gone to Sierra Leone to investigate an abnormal prevalence" of the disease.[1] A month later, the first reports were received. "Research workers on their way to scene" read the *Liverpool Post* on July 7; the "outbreak" was located in the Sierra Leone hinterland and neighboring Guinea. In August, alarming news came from the eastern region of Sierra Leone: "Reports appear

to indicate that the outbreak is assuming the proportion of an epidemic"; 500 cases, all of them potentially fatal, had been discovered during an extensive survey of only 9,500 persons.[2] There were the usual journalists' approximations about African geography: it was written that the disease had "spread from Nigeria and the Gold Coast along the hinterland and Sierra Leone and into...Sénégal." There were the usual heroes, like the MRC researcher Dr. Lourie, who went onsite alone and set up the first "treatment centers" with very limited means. And there were the first signs of mobilization and hope. "It is anticipated," read the *Liverpool Daily Post*, "that the Sierra

1   *Liverpool Post*, 7 June 1939.

2   *Liverpool Daily Post*, 11 August 1939.

Leone government will organize measures to deal with the epidemic and that more doctors and trained staff will be available. Dispensaries are being set up in the districts worst affected, and it is hoped that use of new drugs will conquer the epidemic."[3]

The results obtained with the experimental drugs in the treatment centers were excellent, "very promising," according to most British newspapers. The drugs were only known by their code names (MB800, MB744). The *Daily Express* published a long story about "Drug X," a secret drug "so hush hush that only…high-up medical experts know its name," which had just been discovered by a public-private partnership between a subsidiary of Sanofi, the MRC, and a major global health research institution. On the field, the trial included 50 to 100 new patients who presented themselves in treatment centers each day; many of them too weak to walk, reported the *Daily Express*. All the specialists interviewed remained cautious until the successful results were announced in New York at the International Congress of Microbiology at the end of the summer.

This outbreak in the Guinea-Sierra Leone transborder region occurred more than 70 years ago, in 1939.[4] The disease was trypanosomiasis, or "sleeping sickness," a parasitic infection transmitted by the tsetse fly, which provokes neuro-psychiatric disorders, cachexia (wasting), and often death. The drugs were pentamidine and propamidine, new molecules of the diamidine family, discovered months earlier at May & Baker, a London-based firm belonging to the Sanofi's French ancestor, Rhone Poulenc, and tested at the Liverpool School of Tropical Medicine and in its colonial outposts. The work done by Lourie and his successors in the Kailahun District was one of the largest clinical trials ever conducted in colonial Africa. It led to the demonstration of the therapeutic efficiency of the diamidines, which counted among the wonder drugs of postwar tropical medicine, and to the extensive documentation of their (quite serious) side effects. The event took place at the outset of the Second World War, in the context of an unprecedented epidemic raging in the Guinea-Sierra Leone-Liberia tripoint zone: the exact area that was the initial focus of the current Ebola epidemic.

It all started in April 1939 with a report from the eastern border of Sierra Leone, sent to London by the director of the Alfred Jones Laboratory in Freetown, a small research laboratory belonging to the Liverpool School: "The situation is as follows: there is a focus…extent not certain, around Dia. The two medical officers who have investigated the area are entirely unreliable but…this situation appears to call for a more careful investigation to determine the incidence of infection and the area of country involved." Responding to the letter, Professor Warrington Yorke, the Dean of the Liverpool School of Tropical Medicine, immediately offered the expertise of the School to the Government of Sierra Leone. "We ought to offer to do a little more to help Sierra Leone…by sending out somebody." Yorke had been supervising laboratory tests on the diamidines, which proved very effective on animals, and he was keen to see them tested on humans. Emmanuel Lourie, a MRC laboratory researcher with no colonial experience, boarded the *Accra* on May 31 carrying batches of the new drugs. Only 15 days later, he began to screen the populations for sleeping sickness cases near Kailahun, at the eastern border of Sierra Leone.

In 1939, the colonial health services in Sierra Leone had absolutely no experience in sleeping sickness control: Lourie, the man in charge, had never worked in Africa. So they consulted the French doctors just across the border in Gueckedou, Guinea. The French colonial doctors considered the fight against sleeping sickness their national specialty; they had organized an impressive service covering the whole territory of French West Africa, with headquarters in Bobo Dioulasso. Their action was based on mobile teams for the screening and treatment of cases with standardized cures based on (Rhone Poulenc) injectable drugs. A network of "segregation camps" was set up for incurable cases and experimental work. In 1939, the Sleeping Sickness Service, nicknamed "La Trypano," already had its dead heroes, its founding myths, and a considerable experience in the bureaucratic management of a continent-wide program, including the training of hundreds of African auxiliaries and the follow-up of millions of patients. The French were more than happy to advise the British. Gaston Muraz, head of the service, personally came to Gueckedou to meet with Lourie, and took him in the field to witness the functioning of a mobile team. He sent hundreds of pages of practical and legal advice to the Sierra Leone government to set up a similar program. The service never materialized on the scale of the Sierra Leone colony, but the "French system" formed the basis of the humanitarian-experimental infrastructure of the 1939 clinical trial in the Kailahun-Koindu area.

Such transborder exchange was not exceptional in colonial medicine: it was indeed constitutive of most programs of disease control in colonial Africa. The circulation of knowledge and knowhow responding to the regional spread of the epidemic, which by the 1940s included the whole forest region of Guinea, Liberia, east Sierra Leone, and the western portion of Ivory Coast. Borders were not an obstacle to medical control; they made it possible.

---

3   *Liverpool Daily Post,* 11 August 1939.

4   My narrative is based on the Liverpool School of Tropical Medicine Archives, LSTM, TM18/3/75/, Sierra Leone. Also see Lachenal (2014).

IT IS A COINCIDENCE, but the spatial overlap between the two epidemics is striking. In Sierra Leone, the "Kissi triangle" was the most affected in 1939 and it is today the "epicenter" of the Ebola epidemic, as CNN wrote in August (Swails and McKenzie 2014). Then and now, the epidemic extended all through the Kissi country, across the borders of Guinea and Liberia, and south towards Kenema and west into the Kono District. The superposition of the two maps is not an accident or an artifact of historical research.

It points to the simple fact that the global health infrastructure now at work in the region has a long history: a history of treatment centers, of catastrophic mortality and saved lives, of people seeking or fleeing medical teams, and of medical heroes and foreign journalists, which started long before this summer of 2014. Anthropologists now working in the area might be able to tell us whether this past is present in memories: if this history of medical miracles and accidents had something to do (or not) with

are giving second lives to biopolitical infrastructures in many places of the world, such as leper stations becoming jails; TB sanatoriums becoming psychiatric hospitals; and sleeping sickness camps becoming Ebola centers.

The coincidence also points to the specific ecology of the transborder region. The fact that the zone is literally occupied by frontiers has been a dramatic factor in the Ebola outbreak. Frontiers, though largely irrelevant to kinship and social networks, stimulated the opportunistic movement of people (for trade or protection, for example) in the post-conflict context; in the current epidemic, they have complicated access to treatment, contact-tracing, and international coordination.[6] The same frontier ecology played a major role in the 1940–1950 sleeping sickness epidemic, when French reports noted that Liberians crossed the border to access to the French drugs, or that entire villages fled the medical teams by going "on the other side." It is a cliché to say that African frontiers are zones of economic marginalization and opportunity, of

Such transborder exchange was not exceptional in colonial medicine: it was indeed constitutive of most programs of disease control in colonial Africa. … Borders were not an obstacle to medical control; they made it possible.

the sometimes very tense encounters between medical teams and populations in the current outbreak.

It also reveals that several elements of the very infrastructure used in the current response are inherited from the years of trypanosomiasis control. In Sierra Leone, Médecins San Frontières (MSF; Doctors Without Borders) established one of its most important treatment centers in Kailahun (in a site away from the main hospital [see Open Street Map] to avoid disruption of its functioning); in their era, the British doctors followed a similar logic when they chose Kailahun as their base, and "recommended that the Leper Settlement at Kailahun be taken over by Government and maintained as a centre for sleeping sickness cases…." The head researcher of the trial, Emmanuel Lourie eventually settled in Koindu, a smaller locality further north that is heavily stricken by Ebola these days, where MSF has installed a referral center. I wonder if the same buildings are being reused, as it is the case in Gueckedou, Guinea, where MSF has installed its large treatment center in the old premises of the French Sleeping Sickness Service, still known locally as "La Trypano." I don't know about the precise geography of the Ebola response installations in Macenta and Nzérékoré, but these two Guinean towns also had large logistics bases for the colonial sleeping sickness service of French West Africa (the SGHMP) up until the late 1950s.[5] Such reconversions are not surprising; the logics of spatial relegation

instability and insecurity, of state absence and state violence; the "tripoint" nature of the region adds a factor of multiplication, as evidenced by the recent history of conflicts and refugee movements. Food insecurity—a major matter of concern in the current situation—was also a major issue at the time of the sleeping sickness epidemic. Lourie in 1942 thought malnutrition explained the severity of toxic accidents following treatment in Kailahun: "The patients were mainly of the Kissi tribe, of a very poor and undernourished type. Their diets consist of little else than rice and they are regularly subject to a severe 'hungry season' during the months preceding the annual rice harvest. The 'hungry season' of 1940 was, for a number of reasons, particularly serious, amounting practically to a period of true famin." (Lourie, 1942)

What is *specific* in the emergence of the West African Ebola epidemic has certainly more to do with cross-border connections than with cross-species transmissions. Most commentaries concerning the "ground zero" of the current Ebola outbreak, echoing the dominant scientific framing of Ebola as a zoonotic disease, have insisted on human–bat contact implicitly understood as abnormal and dangerous (and disgusting). As Mike McGovern (2014) has pointed out, the emphasis on bushmeat as the original source of the virus obscures the historically produced material conditions that have enabled its massive and unprecedented spread among humans. Instead of exoticizing

---

5   On sleeping sickness in the area of Gueckedou, Macenta, and Nzérékoré, and the French trials of the diamidines, see Diallo (1951).

6   For a spatial analysis of the current Ebola epidemic in Sierra Leone, see Richards et al. (2014).

a form of cross-species pathogen sharing (which is totally banal in itself), the current Ebola epidemic asks us to put the emphasis (both in terms of control and research) on the decisive role of the environmental, political, and historical conditions that rolled out the red carpet for virus transmission among humans, including the specific spatial patterns of human mobility in the region.

It is worth going back to the work of Maximilien Sorre, an early figure of French biogeography who had a major influence on ecological science in France. Writing in 1943 (at the moment of the Sierra Leone outbreak) and taking as an example the geography of African sleeping sickness, Sorre insisted that infectious diseases had to be understood at the scale of a "biological unit of a superior order: the pathogen complex...including, with man and the causal agent of the disease, its vectors and all the beings which condition or compromise their existence" (1943:293). The notion of "pathogen complex" led Sorre to propose one the first ecological understanding of infectious diseases, which gave a central role to anthropogenic ecosystems linked to agriculture, migration, irrigation or public works; it inspired medical historian Mirko Grmek's concept of "pathocenosis," which referred to specific associations of environments, human societies, animal species, and diseases (Grmek 1969).

The Liberia–Guinea–Sierra Leone tripoint may be seen as a specific transborder "pathocenosis": a bio-political environment producing rubber, diamonds, parasitic diseases, emerging viruses, and war injuries. To my knowledge, neither Sorre nor Grmek thought of frontiers as defining specific "pathogen complexes." Interestingly, one of the first reflections on frontiers-as-pathological-environments in Africa was written in 1958 by Bernard B. Waddy, a Gold Coast colonial doctor with a long experience of trypanosomiasis control and a long history of interaction and friendship with the French doctors across the border. This is not the first time that frontiers have played an important role in the making of an Ebola epidemic, as Célia Gasquet showed in her work on the 2001–2002 outbreak at the Gabon-Congo border (Gasquet 2010). In the West African tripoint zone, or at the Thailand-Cambodia border where artemisin-resistant *Plasmodium falciparum* were detected in the summer of 2014 (Packard 2014), frontier environments shape the global landscape of emergence of disease and drug resistance.

New epidemics seem to call for historical research: they open new perspectives on the past just as they require new critical engagements (Fee and Fox 1988). They call for "histories of the present" which can help question the taken-for-grantedness of our categories and responses. What histories does the Ebola epidemic ask for? What are its urgent pasts? It could be, as some suggested, the 1980-1990's experience of structural adjustment and health "reform" or, closer to us, the last decade of "pandemic preparedness" fireworks and failures--and the sedimented traces of colonial biopolitics in the area. ◾

GUILLAUME LACHENAL *is Lecturer in history of medicine at the Université Paris Diderot. He is the author of* Le médicament qui devait sauver l'Afrique *(La Découverte, 2014)*

BIBLIOGRAPHY

Diallo, J. 1951. "Résultats de la chimioprophylaxie par les diamidines dans le secteur spécial No 3, à Gueckedou-Kissidougou (Guinee)." *Bulletin de la Societe de pathologie exotique et de ses filiales*, 44(1–2):93-103.

Fee, Elizabeth, and Daniel M. Fox, eds. 1988. *AIDS: The burdens of history*. Berkeley, CA: University of California Press.

Gasquet, Célia. 2010. "Ébola au Gabon et au Congo: Logiques transfrontalières de survie et gestion transnationale de la crise épidémique de 2001-2002." In *Frontières et santé: Genèses et maillages des réseaux transfrontaliers*, edited by F. Moulle and S. Duhamel. Paris: Géographie et Culture, L'Harmattan.

Grmek, Mirko. 1969. "Préliminaire d'une étude historique des maladies." *Annales ESC*, 24:1437-1483.

Lachenal, Guillaume. 2014. *Le médicament qui devait sauver l'Afrique*. Paris : La Découverte.

McGovern, Mike. 2014. "Bushmeat and the Politics of Disgust." *Fieldsights - Hot Spots, Cultural Anthropology Online*, October 07, 2014, http://www.culanth.org/fieldsights/588-bushmeat-and-the-politics-of-disgust

Richards, Paul, Joseph Amara, Mariane C. Ferme, Prince Kamara, EstherMokuwa, Amara Idara Sheriff, Roland Suluku, and Maarten Voors. 2014. "Social Pathways for Ebola Virus Disease in Rural Sierra Leone, and some Implications for Containment." *PLoS Neglected Tropical Diseases*, October 31. Available at http://blogs.plos.org/speakingofmedicine/2014/10/31/social-pathways-ebola-virus-disease-rural-sierra-leone-implications-containment/.

Packard, Randall. 2014. "The Origins of Antimalarial-Drug Resistance." *New England Journal of Medicine*, 371(5):397-399.

Sorre, Maximilien. 1943. *Les fondements biologiques de la géographie humaine: Essai d'une écologie de l'homme*. Paris: Armand Colin.

Swails, Brent, and David McKenzie. 2014. "Treating Ebola in Sierra Leone: 'We Are Two Steps Behind.'" *CNN*, August 9. Available at http://edition.cnn.com/2014/08/08/world/africa/ebola-sierra-leone-mckenzie-swails/.

Waddy, Bernard B. 1958. "Frontiers and Disease in West Africa." *The Journal of Tropical Medicine and Hygiene*, 61(4):100-107.

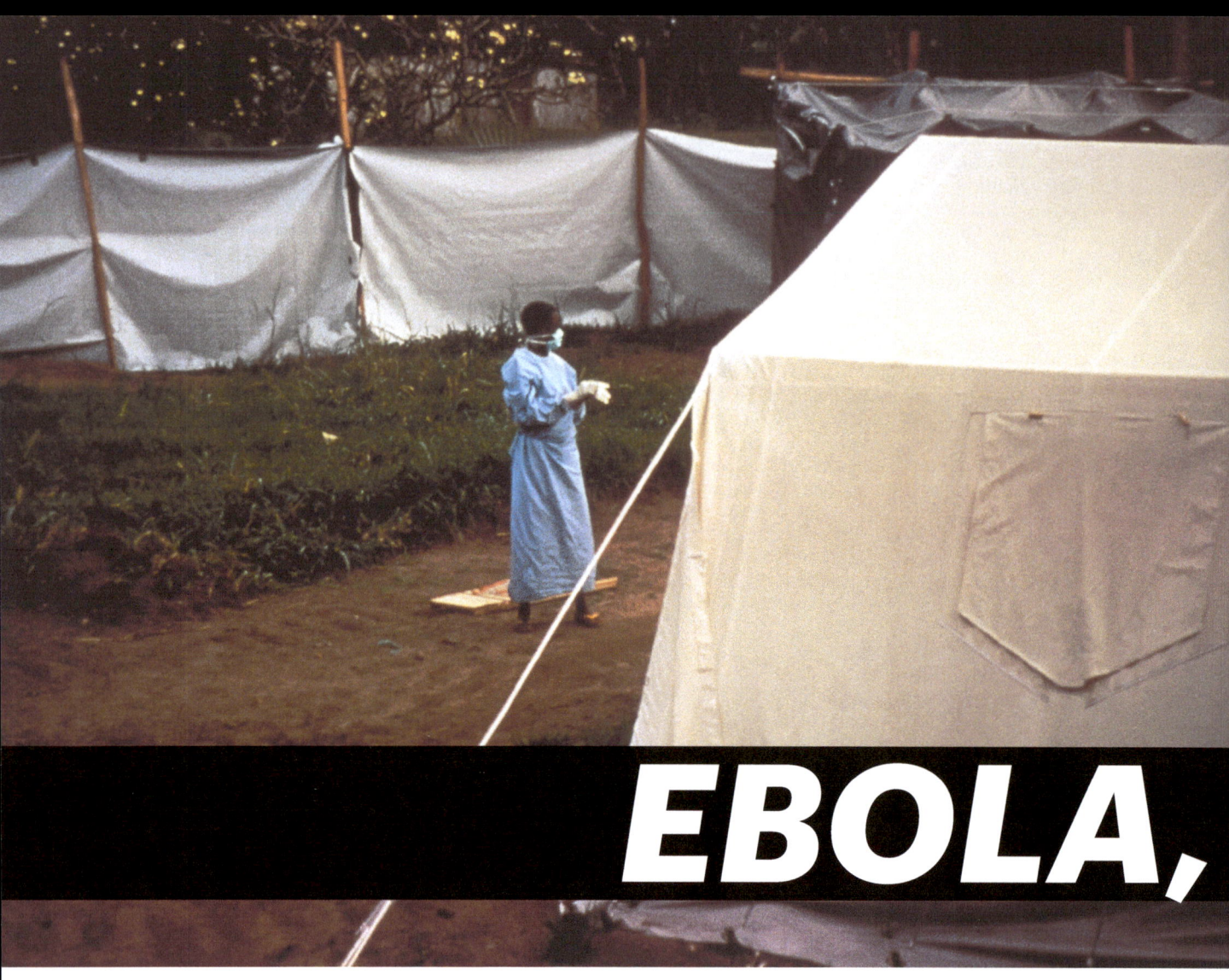

EBOLA,

Nicholas B. King looks back at the dialectics of confidence and paranoia in the Ebola outbreaks of 1995 and 2014.

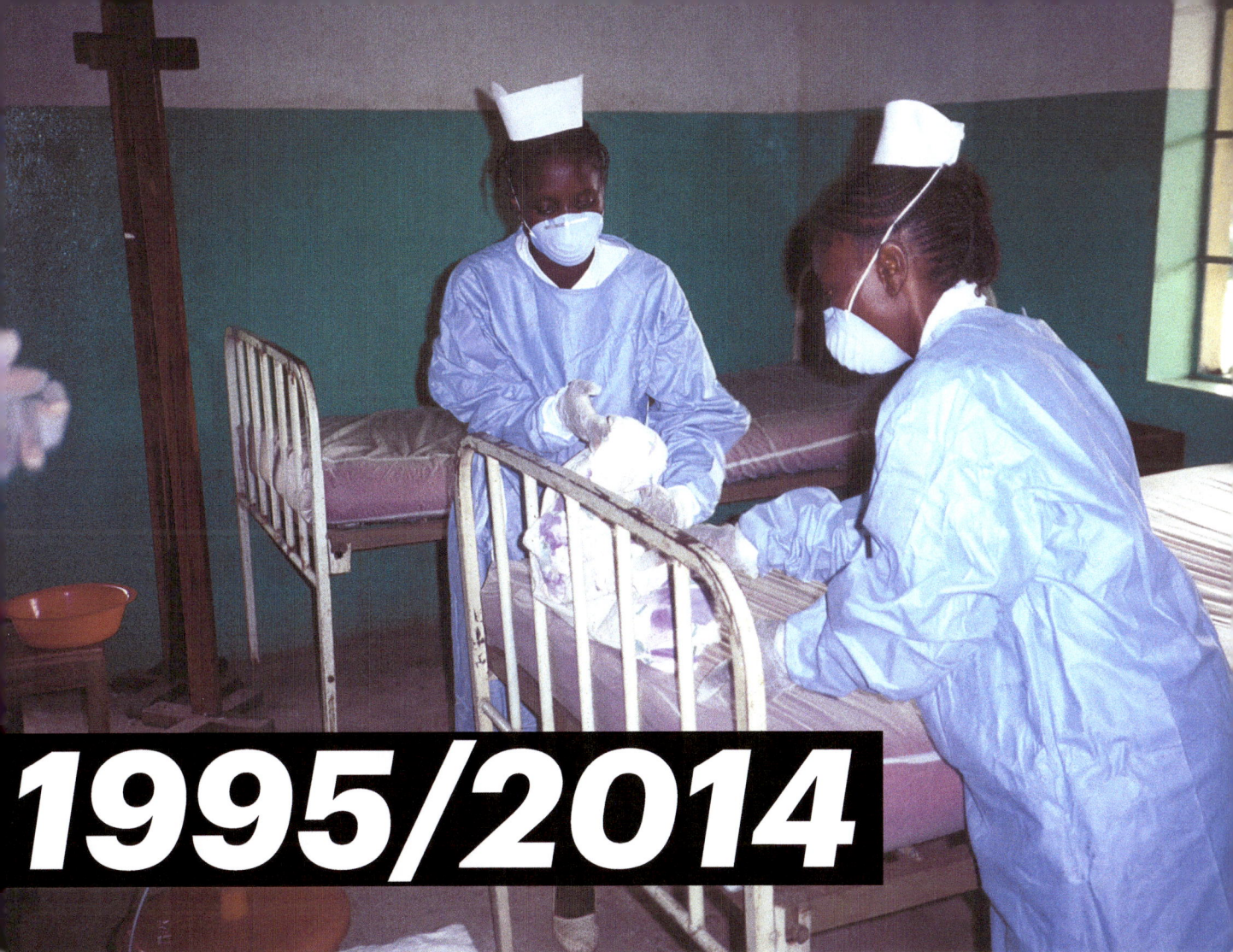

1995/2014

EBOLA 2014

Infectious disease in poor African nations rarely generates the kind of sustained attention that the 2014 Ebola outbreak event has. Lassa fever, a viral hemorrhagic illness estimated to infect roughly 300,000 and kill 5,000 every year in West Africa, hardly receives any attention at all.[1] Nevertheless, in a recent Gallup poll, Americans ranked Ebola third when asked to name "the most urgent health problem facing the country at the current time," just behind access to health care, and ahead of cancer and obesity.

The disjuncture between the actual threat posed by Ebola in North America, and the apparent fear it has generated, has itself become an object of intense scrutiny. As media coverage of cases in West Africa and North America has grown, so too has the proliferation of contrarian voices taking

North Americans to task for being unnecessarily afraid of the virus. Social media is awash with listicles—including Salon's "6 things Americans should fear more than Ebola" (Schwartz 2014), Humanosphere's "5 diseases Americans should fear way more than Ebola" (Murphy 2014), and Cracked's "5 Reasons America Can Calm the F#@% Down About Ebola" (Bell and Tashjian 2014)—admonishing readers for worrying about Ebola rather than comparatively more prevalent threats to health.

The discourse of disjuncture is not limited to popular media. Public health law expert Lawrence O. Gostin (2014) argues that the United States and Europe have "grossly overreacted" with "panicked responses" that ultimately divert attention from the correct response: improving basic health care infrastructure in West Africa. Similarly, in a widely distributed *London Review of Books* essay, anthropologist Paul Farmer laments that "the cycle of fear

1 See the Viral Hemorrhagic Fever Consortium's website on Lassa fever at http://vhfc.org/lassa_fever.

and stigma, amped up by the media, will continue to spiral, even though there's little doubt that the epidemic will be contained in the US, which has the staff, stuff, space and systems" that are lacking in the countries hardest-hit by the Ebola outbreak (Farmer 2014). Under the headline "Canada's response to Ebola driven by fear, not evidence," a trio of Canadian physicians calls Canadian travel restrictions "illogical and anti-public health... likely to cause more harm than good" (Sharma et al. 2014).

While the substance of these critiques is likely correct—Ebola poses little threat to the healthy and wealthy citizens of North America—in this essay I am interested in their form, which illustrates what we might call a dialectic of confidence and paranoia. This dialectic plays out at the level of both lay and expert discourse, alternating between reporting that amplifies the threat of Ebola and critical commentary claiming a more accurate and level-headed risk assessment. This reflexive approach to risk, simultaneously producing knowledge about Ebola and critiquing the conditions of that knowledge's production, circulation, and consumption, is a hallmark of modern risk communication. With respect to Ebola, its roots stretch back at least 20 years.

EBOLA 1995

Ebola first came to widespread attention for North American audiences in September 1994 with publication of Richard Preston's *The Hot Zone*, which was based on a 1992 *New Yorker* article. In riveting prose, Preston described an outbreak of Ebola hemorrhagic fever among a shipment of laboratory monkeys at a primate quarantine unit maintained by Hazelton Research Products in late 1989, which resulted in the euthanization of several hundred monkeys and four subclinical infections among humans. A multiweek national bestseller, the book garnered Preston a reported $3 million advance for his next book, numerous awards, and a mention among the *American Scientist*'s list of "100 or so Books that Shaped a Century of Science" (Morrison and Morrison 1999). Preston's work also inspired intense interest in the culture industries—Preston has claimed that "within two months of the publication of my piece, 20 unauthorized screenplays thudded onto the desks of producers all over Hollywood" (Fine 1995:4D)—resulting in several films and bestselling books on Ebola-like viruses.

As Preston's book was making its way down the bestseller list, its alarmist speculations appeared to find justification in real-world events. For three weeks in May 1995, news media issued daily reports on an outbreak of Ebola in Kikwit, Zaire (now Democratic Republic of Congo). Major magazines, including *Newsweek*, *Time*, and *The Economist*, published cover stories on the "Killer Virus"; network news programs such as ABC's *Nightline* devoted special episodes to the outbreak; and CNN

aired a special report on "The Apocalypse Bug."

The Kikwit outbreak eventually killed fewer than 300, and no cases were ever reported in North America. While coverage ebbed quickly, the combination of Preston's fictional account and a real-world outbreak fixed Ebola as an emblematic disease. A Google *n*-gram shows mentions of Ebola increasing eightfold and subsequently flattening out at the higher level after 1994 (Figure 1). Five years after the events in Kikwit, a *U.S. News and World Report* poll asked which presidential candidate would better respond to nine national crises,

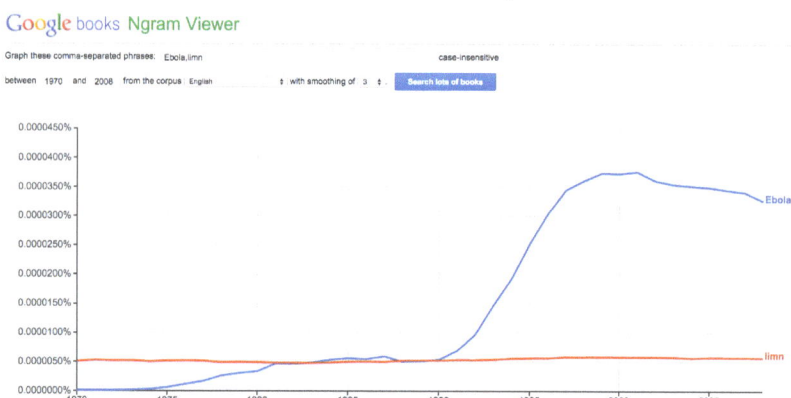

Google *n*-gram for "Ebola". The *n*-gram charts frequencies of any word or short sentence in books.

including "a stock market crash," "a US is attacked by another country," and "Ebola virus spread across the country" (voters preferred Al Gore over George W. Bush by a 42% to 31% margin for the last case) (Whitman 2000).

Coverage of the Kikwit outbreak drew a backlash comparable to the listicles of 2014. The July 1995 issue of *The New Republic* featured a critical article by Malcolm Gladwell, trumpeted on the cover as "Paranoia Strikes Deep. Ebola, *Outbreak*, *The Hot Zone* and the new panic about plagues" (Figure 2). Arguing that Americans were "in the grip of paranoia about viruses and diseases," he argued that "it is because of the success of *The Hot Zone* that *Outbreak* was made, that the Ebola outbreak in Zaire was covered as feverishly as it was, that the idea of killer viruses has achieved such sudden prominence. In the epidemic of virus paranoia, *The Hot Zone* is patient zero" (Gladwell 1995:39).

Four years later, journalism scholar Susan Moeller devoted a quarter of her book *Compassion Fatigue: How the Media Sell Disease, Famine, War, and Death* to a critique of Ebola coverage. Arguing that the American public suffered from an inability to sustain concern about specific, long-term, or low-intensity crises or social problems, a malady she called "compassion fatigue," she argued that "it's the media that are at fault. How they typically cover crises helps us to feel overstimulated and bored all at once." Moeller saved her harshest criticism for "the late-20th-century phenomenon of the melding of news and entertainment,

The New Republic, July 1995.

the vanishing boundaries between news-worthy events and celebrity spectacle" (Moeller 1999:34).

Two years later, when 32-year-old Colette Matshimoseka fell ill after arriving in Canada from the Democratic Republic of Congo, suspicions that she might have Ebola sparked widespread media coverage. In response, *Toronto Star* science correspondent Leslie Papp presented a now-familiar critique of the "outbreak of hype":

> Among mass killers it's more Mickey Mouse than Hannibal Lecter, but the Ebola virus still sends shivers through North Americans—thanks to Hollywood. Pop culture, rather than lab cultures, is at the root of an Ebola scare that rippled across the continent this week from the unlikely epicentre of Henderson General Hospital in Hamilton... Ebola is different, not because it's more dangerous than other viruses. It's the one that's gone Hollywood... The virus has been the subject of scores of sensational articles, books, and, above all, movies. Filtered through Hollywood's carnival lens, it looks disturbingly apocalyptic—a mass killer—as easy to catch as the common cold and capable of rapidly spreading across the continent (Papp 2001:NE03).

These analyses were at best oversimplifications; concern over new infectious diseases during the

Outbreak (Warner Bros., 1995) starred Cuba Gooding Jr. (left), Kevin Spacey (center), and Dustin Hoffman (right).

1990s owed a great deal to a calculated public campaign about "emerging diseases" by scientists and policymakers (King 2004). Appearing in the same year as Preston's original article, the 1992 Institute of Medicine report *Emerging Infections: Microbial Threats to Health in the United States* (Lederberg et al. 1992) argued that Americans should be far less sanguine about the threat posed by novel infections, including Ebola. Nevertheless, between 1995 and 2001, critical reflections on the dialectic of confidence and paranoia presented a stark opposition: confident, measured scientific understanding of the true threat of Ebola on one side; paranoid fears stoked by mass media and the culture industries on the other.

CONFIDENCE, PARANOIA, AND THE RISK COMMUNICATION INDUSTRY

While superficially similar, the 1995 and 2014 versions of the dialectic of confidence and paranoia differ in one key way. In the 1990s, critics were most concerned with the blurring of boundaries between fact and fiction in coverage of Ebola and other emerging diseases. Nostalgic for an age in which clear firewalls separated journalism from the culture industries, critics lashed out at both the structural consolidation of entertainment and news media, and the practical intermixing of fact and fiction in newspapers, TV, film, and especially the nascent World Wide Web. According to the critics, American consumers that had come to depend on these firewalls to filter their understandings of risk were now threatened with a confusing and corrupting merger of fantasy and reality.

In 2014, the dialectic of confidence and paranoia looks different to the "risk experts" seeking to explain public irrationality. Gone is the faith in a rational individual threatened by confusing or manipulative reporting. In its place are decisionmakers hampered not by the media but by their own brains. Far from rational consumers, human beings (not just North Americans) are instead statistically illiterate, prone to irrational misjudgment of the relevance and magnitude of risks, subject to cognitive biases and framing effects, and dependent on premodern heuristics ill-suited to the complexities of twenty-first-century life. Whereas in 1995 experts were afraid that otherwise rational citizens were led astray by media-driven paranoia, in 2014 experts warned against misplaced confidence in an illusory human rationality.

What explains this shift? In the 20 years since Kikwit, cognitive psychology and behavioral economics have called into question humans' ability to reliably interpret, predict, and respond to risk (Ariely 2008, Kahneman 2011). The dominant narrative now is not one of rational humans corrupted by inaccurate reporting, but rather "predictably irrational" humans whose corruption is innate, hardwired into brains produced by millions of years of evolution that have yet to catch up with our complex, modern risk environment. Inherent human fallibility about risk is the root cause of everything ranging from vaccine refusal to low organ donation rates, low participation in 401Ks to ignorance of the "black swans" responsible for economic crises.

Tracking the contours of human fallibility, a cottage industry of journalists and academic experts have set themselves the task of explaining just how consistently wrong we are about just about every risk. as reflected in the titles of two popularizations, Dan Gardner's *Risk: Why We Fear the Things We Shouldn't—And Put Ourselves in Greater Danger* and Barry Glassner's *The Culture of Fear: Why Americans Are Afraid of the Wrong Things: Crime, Drugs, Minorities, Teen Moms, Killer Kids, Mutant Microbes, Plane Crashes, Road Rage, & So Much More.* The common thread running through this type of work is that imperfect humans cannot be relied upon to make good decisions, and must be supplemented by carefully

CNN, October 2014.

In 1995 experts were afraid that otherwise rational citizens were led astray by media–driven paranoia. In 2014 experts warned against misplaced confidence in an illusory human rationality.

designed choice architecture to guide us, or supplanted entirely by expert systems to do the deciding for us.

In 1995, arbiters of the distinction between rational and irrational risk perception criticized manipulation of essential human subjectivity by nefarious outside forces. Gladwell, Moeller, and Papp criticized media for exaggeration and blurring fact/fiction boundaries, but left intact the possibility that responsible media, disseminating objective science to rational individuals, could produce good decisions. They thus called for reform of existing communication infrastructure, to ensure that confident rational humans were not duped into paranoia.

In 2014, a new set of arbiters preaches management rather than structural reform, advising us to look to outside forces to manipulate us into better decisions. In doing so, twenty-first-century experts in risk communication, behavioral economics, and cognitive psychology carve out a novel managerial space. If individuals cannot be relied upon to be correctly confident *or* paranoid, then they require constant expert supervision. The ultimate source of rationality thus is located not in individual humans, but rather the distributed architecture of risk management, endlessly channeling our atavistic human brains into productive decisions. ■

NICHOLAS B. KING *is an associate professor in the Biomedical Ethics Unit, and an associate member of the Department of Epidemiology, Biostatistics, and Occupational Health at McGill*

University.

REFERENCES

Ariely, Daniel. 2008. *Predictably Irrational: The Hidden Forces That Shape Our Decisions.* New York: Harper Collins.

Bell, David Christopher, and Chris Tashjian. 2014. "5 Reasons America Can Calm the F#@% Down about Ebola." *Cracked,* November 8. Available at http://www.cracked.com/quick-fixes/why-americans-need-to-calm-f234025-down-about-ebola/.

Farmer, Paul. 2014. "Diary." *London Review of Books,* 36(20):38-39. Available at http://www.lrb.co.uk/v36/n20/paul-farmer/diary.

Fine, Marshall. 1995. "A Contagious Fascination with Infections: An 'Outbreak' Sweeps through Hollywood." *USA Today, Feburary 28,* 4D.

Gardner, Dan. 2008. *Risk: Why We Fear the Things We Shouldn't—And Put Ourselves in Greater Danger.* London, UK: Virgin Books.

Gladwell, Malcolm. 1995. "The Plague Year." *The New Republic,* July 17, 24, pp. 38-46

Glassner, Barry. 1999. *The Culture of Fear: Why Americans Are Afraid of the Wrong Things: Crime, Drugs, Minorities, Teen Moms, Killer Kids, Mutant Microbes, Plane Crashes, Road Rage, & So Much More.* New York: Basic Books.

Gostin, Lawrence O. 2014. "Ebola and Beyond." *Project Syndicate,* November 19. Available at http://www.project-syndicate.org/commentary/ebola-international-response-by-lawrence-o--gostin-2014-11.

Kahneman, Daniel. 2011. *Thinking, Fast and Slow.* New York: Random House.

King, Nicholas B. 2004. "The Scale Politics of Emerging Diseases." *Osiris,* 19:62-76.

Lederberg, Joshua, Robert E. Shope, and Stanley C. Oaks. 1992. *Emerging Infections: Microbial Threats to Health in the United States.* Washington, DC: National Academy Press.

Moeller, Susan D. 1999. *Compassion Fatigue: How the Media Sell Disease, Famine, War, and Death.* New York: Routledge.

Morrison, Philip, and Phyllis Morrison. 1999. "100 or So Books That Shaped a Century of Science." *American Scientist,* 87: 543-553.

Murphy, Tom. 2014. "5 Diseases Americans Should Fear Way More than Ebola." *Humanosphere,* August 5. Available at http://www.humanosphere.org/global-health/2014/08/5-diseases-americans-fear-way-ebola/.

Papp, Leslie. 2001. "The Real Outbreak Has Been...Hype." *The Toronto Star,* February 10, p. NE03.

Preston, Richard. 1994. *The Hot Zone.* New York: Random House.

Schwartz, Larry. 2014. "6 Things Americans Should Fear More than Ebola." *Salon,* October 17. Available at http://www.salon.com/2014/10/17/6_things_americans_should_fear_more_than_ebola_partner/.

Sharma, Malika, Ross Upshur, and James Orbinski. 2014. "Canada's Response to Ebola Driven by Fear, Not Evidence." *The Globe and Mail,* November 13. Available at http://www.theglobeandmail.com/globe-debate/canadas-response-to-ebola-driven-by-fear-not-evidence/article21570606/.

Whitman, David. 2000. "Unhappy and up for Grabs." *U.S. News and World Report,* November 6, p. 22.

ABOVE: The executive board room of the World Health Organization.
PHOTO BY THORKILD TYLLESKAR (LICENSED UNDER THE CREATIVE COMMONS ATTRIBUTION-SHARE ALIKE 3.0 UNPORTED LICENSE)

TWO STATES OF EMERGENCY
EBOLA 2014

Andrew Lakoff revisits the received wisdom that the WHO was slow to respond. Slow to respond to what exactly?

I n the late summer and early fall of 2014, as the Ebola epidemic spun seemingly out of control in West Africa and threatened to spread globally, multiple observers began to weigh in on where the failure of response lay. The international response had been "slow and feeble," wrote two leaders of Médecins Sans Frontières (MSF). "It can equally be defined as irresponsible" (Nierle and Jochum 2014). World Bank President Jim Yong Kim noted multiple lapses: health care systems had not been put in place, monitoring was not conducted when the first cases appeared, and there was no organized response. "We were tested by Ebola and we failed," he concluded (Elliot 2014). The diagnosis of failure, of course, assumes a locus of responsibility. From this perspective, the disaster was neither unforeseen nor uncontrollable: the epidemic was not an unavoidable danger but a manageable risk, and therefore it demands a retrospective accounting.

The World Health Organization (WHO) received much of the criticism; the organization learned of the outbreak in March but did not declare an official emergency until August, and even then had difficulty galvanizing an intensive international response. The WHO "should be the global leader" in directing and coordinating international health efforts, argued two legal scholars, but the organization's institutional weakness and lack of control over its resources had made it unable to lead global health response: "Failures in leadership have allowed a preventable disease to spin out of control, with vast harms to social order and human dignity" (Gostin and Friedman 2014). Journalist Laurie Garrett was even more scathing: "The WHO's response has been abysmal. It's just shameful." In defense of its leaders, however, she also noted "WHO is just a shadow of its former financial self" because of the changing priorities of its member nations (Renwick 2014).[1]

Meanwhile, WHO was already engaged in critical self-scrutiny. In October, the Associated Press reported that an internal WHO investigation revealed that the agency had "missed chances to prevent Ebola from spreading soon after it was first diagnosed in Liberia, Sierra Leone and Guinea last spring, citing factors such as incompetent staff and a lack of information," but also the inappropriate application of response methods that had been successful in other settings to the region of the 2014 outbreak (Cheng and Geller 2014).[2]

In this essay I offer a somewhat different interpretation of the "failure." Rather than focusing on a lack of resources or organizational weakness, I suggest that the failure was one of administrative imagination: global health authorities did not conceptualize Ebola as the source of a potentially catastrophic global epidemic, but rather categorized it as a disease that could be managed via localized humanitarian care combined with straightforward public health techniques. I focus on a moment that looks, in retrospect, like one of lost opportunity: in late March and early April, when the outbreak was first reported to WHO. Why, a number of critics have asked, did the agency not immediately declare a global health emergency and seek to galvanize international response (see Fearnley, this issue)? Why did it wait until five months later to do so, and more than a month after MSF warned that the outbreak was "totally out of control"?

An initial way to pose the question might be: To what extent, as of spring 2014, did the Ebola outbreak present a global health emergency? It is useful to begin with a timeline of the early stages of international response. In mid-March, MSF discovered suspected Ebola cases near its malaria clinic in Guéckédou, Guinea. Within a week, MSF launched an emergency response: doctors, nurses, logisticians, and hygiene and sanitation experts were sent to Guinea; isolation units were set up in Guéckédou and elsewhere; and 33 tons of supplies (such as personal protective equipment and palliative medicines) were shipped to Guinea from warehouses in Belgium and France. This was an event for which MSF was well prepared. As Peter Redfield notes in this issue, MSF had lengthy experience with prior Ebola outbreaks and was the only organization with the personnel, equipment, and treatment protocols available for rapid response to this one.

On March 25, the Guinean Ministry of Health officially notified WHO of the outbreak, reporting 86 suspected cases and 60 deaths. Such notification pointed toward the potential declaration by the WHO Director-General of a "Public Health Emergency of International Concern" (PHEIC), an alert that puts into motion the administrative mechanism of emergency response that is at the heart of WHO's "global public health security" system (see Collier and Lakoff 2008).[3] This system, laid out in the revised International Health Regulations (IHR; WHO 2005), is designed to ensure continued state sovereignty over public health response to an outbreak while at the same time regulating state actions to minimize disruption of the global economy and ensuring that international health authorities can monitor and seek to minimize the

---

1   "The WHO's legislative body, the World Health Assembly, has consistently voted to downgrade the institution's capacity to deal with outbreaks and infectious disease in favor of increasing commitment to noncommunicable disease programs such as cancer and heart disease" (Renwick 2014).

2   "Its own experts failed to grasp that traditional infectious disease containment methods wouldn't work in a region with porous borders and broken health systems, the report found" (Cheng and Geller 2014).

3   A "Public Health Emergency of International Concern" is defined in the 2005 IHR as an "extraordinary event which is determined...(i) to constitute a public health risk to other States through the international spread of disease and (ii) to potentially require a coordinated international response" (WHO 2005).

circulation of the disease. Thus, within the IHR framework, the declaration of a PHEIC points toward a WHO role of coordination and collaboration with presumably functioning national public health systems, and toward an intensive effort to mobilize international assistance.[4]

However, unlike the outbreak of a novel strain of influenza in 2009, the detection of Ebola in the spring of 2014 did not automatically provoke such a declaration. In the prior two decades, Ebola had undergone a conceptual mutation: it was no longer the novel and fearsome virus that helped spark attention and resources to the phenomenon of "emerging infectious disease" in the late 1980s and early 1990s (see King, this issue). By 2014, global health authorities approached its detection with relative confidence. Its pattern of transmission was understood; methods of containment had been developed and standardized. In more than a dozen outbreaks since its initial discovery in 1976, the disease had never killed more than a few hundred people.

However, there were early indications that this event might be different. At the end of March, MSF described the outbreak as one of "unprecedented" magnitude in Guinea, with cases also reported in Liberia. MSF Director Bruno Jochum reported that the disease "had spread to several places and to a large city," making it "an exceptional event for an Ebola outbreak up until today" (Samb 2014). Despite these worrisome signs, Jochum lamented, the international response had so far been "minimal." In contrast, a WHO spokesman sought to assuage public concern, emphasizing that the event should not be considered an "epidemic" but was rather a "relatively small" outbreak in comparison with previous outbreaks (Samb 2014).[5]

Like MSF, WHO was quickly on the ground in Guinea. After its laboratories confirmed the reported cases, the agency deployed teams to the field "to strengthen surveillance, sensitize and educate the public, manage cases and implement appropriate infection prevention and control measures in health facilities and communities affected" (WHO 2014a). An internal situation report from April 2014 (WHO 2014c) describes a WHO "surge" in West Africa of more than 50 staff members as well as members of the

Global Outbreak Alert and Response Network (GOARN) "in accordance with the grading of the outbreak as a grade 2 emergency under the WHO Emergency Response Framework."[6] On the response framework's scale of 1 to 3, a grade 2 emergency indicated an "event with moderate public health consequences," requiring a moderate response from health authorities (WHO 2013:19). The framework is a form of technocratic triage: In a world suffused with emergencies, decision-makers must have a means for deciding how to allocate scarce resources.[7]

At an April 8 press briefing, WHO Assistant Director-General for Health Security Keiji Fukuda provided an evaluation of the situation. On the one hand, he acknowledged this was "one of the most challenging Ebola outbreaks that we have ever faced," both because of the wide geographic distribution of cases and the level of fear and anxiety the outbreak had provoked (WHO 2014b). On the other hand, he expressed confidence that it would be controlled, given experts' familiarity with the disease: "We know very well how this virus is transmitted, we know the kinds of steps that can be taken to stop the transmission of the virus" (WHO 2014b). It was a straightforward matter of identifying the sick, tracing their contacts, and then taking careful prevention and control measures.[8]

By early May, it seemed that Fukuda's confidence had been warranted: few new cases had been reported in either Guinea or Liberia, though MSF "remain[ed] vigilant," and on May 14, WHO reported that "the outbreak seems to be slowing down" (MSF 2014). A U.S. Centers for Disease Control (CDC) epidemiologist on the scene would later recall: "For most of May, we had no new cases showing up at the treatment centers in Guinea or Liberia, and it was possible to think it might have run its course" (Wieners and Kitamura 2014). In retrospect, however, it is clear that over the next month a second wave of the disease was emerging beyond the view of health authorities. On June 20, an MSF director of operations appealed for help from international health organizations, reporting that the outbreak was "totally out of control" (Gander 2014). On July 11, MSF declared that it was in a "race against time" to stop the spread of the disease in Sierra Leone. And yet the international response remained tepid

---

4   IHR (WHO 2005) states: "If WHO...declares that a public health emergency of international concern is occurring, it may offer... further assistance to the State Party, including an assessment of the severity of the international risk and the adequacy of control measures. Such collaboration may include the offer to mobilize international assistance in order to support the national authorities in conducting and coordinating on-site assessments." The IHR acknowledged that many states lacked the capability for effective emergency health response, but instructed the treaty's signatories to "develop, strengthen, and maintain" such a capacity within five years of the adoption of the regulations—though no funding was allocated for poor countries to do so.

5   Gregory Hartl, the WHO spokesman, was concerned not to overstate the severity of the outbreak: "Ebola already causes enough concern and we need to be very careful about how we characterize something which is up until now an outbreak with sporadic cases" (Samb 2014).

6   Deployments included 52 WHO staff and 22 experts from among its global outbreak and response network (GOARN) partners (WHO 2014c).

7   "Over the decade 2001–2010, an average of more than 700 natural and technological emergencies occurred globally every year, affecting approximately 270 million people and causing over 130 000 deaths annually." Notably, the Emergency Response Framework was adopted (following the U.S. system of incident management) by WHO in 2013, not long after the agency was accused of massive over-reaction to the detection of a different pathogenic threat, A/H1N1 (swine flu), in 2009. See note 10.

8   The April 17 situation report (WHO 2014b) evinced a somewhat more nuanced view of the unfolding situation, pointing to the ways in which this event was in fact unlike prior Ebola outbreaks: it was unfolding in a major city, a number of health workers had been infected, and there had been cross-border transmission of the virus.

How the World Health Organization grades emergencies: The Emergency Response Framework

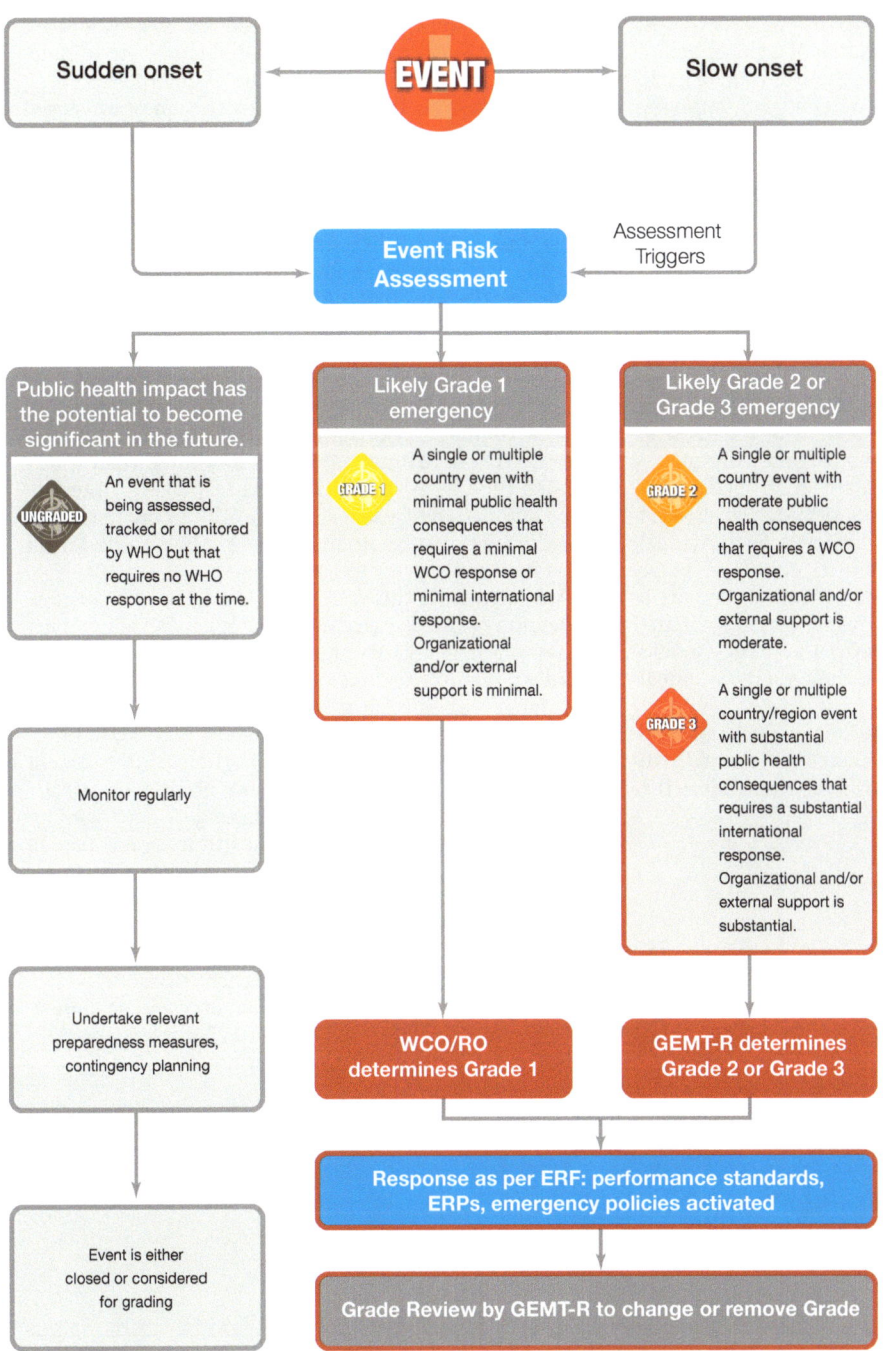

until late July, when two U.S. humanitarian workers came down with the virus and Nigeria announced its first case.[9]

On August 8, 2014, WHO officially declared a PHEIC and established an emergency committee. "The outbreak is moving faster than we can control it," acknowledged Director-General Chan. The declaration of a global health emergency, she said, "will galvanize the attention of leaders of countries at the top level" (WHO 2014d). Replying to the question of what had finally sparked the official declaration, Fukuda pointed to "the identification of the travel-related case, in Nigeria": Ebola was now threatening to spread outside of the immediate region via air travel.

The PHEIC declaration did not by itself direct an infusion of medical care for afflicted populations: rather, WHO recommended that affected states should activate their emergency management mechanisms, engage in risk communication to improve citizens' awareness of the disease, establish secure pipelines of protective medical equipment, and screen travelers for signs of the disease. An ethics committee approved the emergency use of experimental medication (insofar as any such medication could be procured). The emergency declaration did not suspend normal constitutional order (even as individual states did so), nor did it recognize a "stateless" place of complex humanitarian emergency; rather, it was a technocratic classification that activated a system of anticipatory monitoring and response that hopefully would staunch the disease's spread along the circuits of global interconnection.

At its press briefing following the official declaration of emergency, a reporter questioned Director-General Chan about the WHO's belated response. She attributed it to the agency's "stretched" resources:

Q: [G]iven that the first cases I think were reported in Guinea in March, I'm wondering if the response from WHO and others was insufficient at the beginning. Did we not pay enough attention to this? Did we somehow fall down on the job?

A: Let's be very frank. WHO is, at this point in time, or actually, for the last few months, dealing with four Level Three humanitarian crises; they are the biggest, meaning the highest level of crisis, and these are Central African Republic, South Sudan and Syria, and of course, at the same time, we are dealing with three outbreaks, Ebola, MERS-CoVirus, and H7N9, and we have actually mobilized all assets in WHO, and as I said, we are extremely stretched... (WHO 2014d).

And yet, as we have seen, WHO was closely monitoring the outbreak in West Africa in the spring, and had the capacity at that time to coordinate a broader response, or at the very least to galvanize international attention.[10] As significant as the number of emergencies WHO was faced with at the time is its decision—noted above—to initially grade the Ebola outbreak as a "grade 2" emergency.

In conclusion, let us return to the question posed above: Was the outbreak a global health emergency as of April 2014? Is WHO to blame for not responding more aggressively? Perhaps the better question is not whether the initial outbreak should have been considered an emergency, but rather: What kind of emergency was it? If at the time of the outbreak Ebola was best understood as a "neglected disease" that afflicted marginal populations in settings characterized by the absence of state-based health infrastructure, it called for a response from humanitarian biomedicine, concerned with the compassionate alleviation of human suffering regardless of national borders and political conflict. If, alternatively, Ebola was an "emerging disease" that threatened global catastrophe, then it demanded the intensive, coordinated response of international and national health agencies. We can say that some time during the late summer of 2014, Ebola shifted from one state of emergency to another.

Accompanying this shift was a change in the conceptualization of the disease. What changed was not its biological but rather its techno-political meaning. If in the decades prior to the 2014 outbreak Ebola had stabilized as a dangerous but fairly manageable virus, the public health understanding of the disease now had to take other elements into consideration: in particular, the extent to which its virulence and transmissibility—its capacity to provoke a global health emergency—depended on the condition of the local public health infrastructure in which it appeared. ▪

ANDREW LAKOFF is Associate Professor of Sociology and Communication at the University of Southern California. He is the author of Pharmaceutical Reason: Knowledge and Value in Global Psychiatry and co-editor (with Stephen J. Collier) of Biosecurity Interventions: Global Health and Security in Question.

9 At this point, WHO increased its Emergency Response Framework Grade to level 3.

10 Another reason why WHO may have been hesitant to immediately declare a PHEIC is that in 2009 the agency was accused of rashly declaring an emergency very soon after the appearance of H1N1 (swine flu). European critics charged experts on the WHO Emergency Committee with a conflict of interest for encouraging the mass purchase of vaccines that had been developed by companies with whom they had paid consulting relationships. See Lakoff (2013).

BIBLIOGRAPHY

Cheng, Maria, and Adam Geller. 2014. "WHO faulted for Ebola failures as Obama taps czar." *Associated Press*, October 17. Available at http://bigstory.ap.org/article/f0e5fe2192c9433f90159e2efdf76156/who-faulted-ebola-failures-obama-taps-czar

Collier, Stephen J., and Andrew Lakoff. 2008. "The Problem of Securing Health." In *Biosecurity Interventions: Global Health and Security in Question,* edited by Andrew Lakoff and Stephen J. Collier, New York: Columbia University Press, pp. 7-28.

Elliot, Larry. 2014. "Ebola Crisis: Global Response Has 'Failed Miserably', Says World Bank Chief." *The Guardian*, October 9. Available at http://www.theguardian.com/world/2014/oct/08/ebola-crisis-world-bank-president-jim-kim-failure.

Gander, Kashmira. 2014. "Ebola Outbreak: Virus Is 'Totally Out of Control' Warns Doctors Without Borders Medic." *The Independent,* June 20. Available at http://www.independent.co.uk/news/world/africa/ebola-outbreak-virus-is-totally-out-of-control-warns-doctors-without-borders-medic-9553337.html.

Gostin, Lawrence O., and Eric A. Friedman. 2014. "Ebola: A Crisis in Global Health Leadership." *The Lancet*, 384(9951):1323-1325.

Lakoff, Andrew. 2013. "A Dearth of Numbers: The Actuary and the Sentinel in Global Health." *Limn* 3: Sentinel Devices. Available at http://limn.it/a-dearth-of-numbers-the-actuary-and-the-sentinel-in-global-public-health/.

Médecins Sans Frontières (MSF). 2014. "We Cannot Say that the Outbreak Is Over." May 2. Available at http://reliefweb.int/report/guinea/we-cannot-say-ebola-outbreak-over.

Nierle, Thomas, and Bruno Jochum. 2014. "Editorial: Ebola: the failures of the international outbreak response." *Le Temps*, August 29, Available at http://www.msf.org/article/ebola-failures-international-outbreak-response.

Renwick, Danielle. 2014. Interview with Laurie Garrett, September 18, 2014: "Epic Failures Feeding Ebola Crisis." *Council on Foreign Relations*. Available at http://www.cfr.org/public-health-threats-and-pandemics/epic-failures-feeding-ebola-crisis/p33465.

Samb, Saliou. 2014. "WHO Says Guinea Outbreak Small as MSF Slams International Response." Reuters, April 1. Available at http://www.reuters.com/article/2014/04/01/us-guinea-ebola-idUSBREA301X120140401.

Wieners, Brad, and Makiko Kitamura. 2014. "Ebola: Doctors Without Borders Shows How To Manage a Plague." *BloombergBusinessWeek*, November 13. Available at http://www.businessweek.com/articles/2014-11-13/ebola-doctors-without-borders-shows-how-to-manage-a-plague.

World Health Organization (WHO). 2005. *International Health Regulations (2nd edition).* Geneva, Switzerland: WHO.

———. 2013. *Emergency Response Framework.* Geneva, Switzerland: WHO.

———. 2014a. "Ebola virus disease in Guindea. (Situation as of 25 March 2014)." March 25. Available at http://www.afro.who.int/en/clusters-a-programmes/dpc/epidemic-a-pandemic-alert-and-response/outbreak-news/4065-ebola-virus-disease-in-guinea-25-march-2014.html

———. 2014b. "Ebola Outbreak Guinea Presser." April 8. Available at http://www.who.int/mediacentre/multimedia/Ebola_outbreak_Guinea_transcript_08APR2014.pdf.

———. 2014c. "Situation Report 2 Ebola Virus Disease, West Africa, 17 April 2014." Available at http://www.afro.who.int/en/clusters-a-programmes/dpc/epidemic-a-pandemic-alert-and-response/sitreps/4102-sitrep-2-ebola-virus-disease-west-africa-17-april-2014.html.

———. 2014d. "WHO Virtual Press Conference Following the Meeting of the International Health Regulations Emergency Committee Regarding the 2014 Ebola Outbreak in West Africa." August 8. Available at http://www.who.int/mediacentre/multimedia/2014/who-ebola-outbreak-08aug2014.pdf?ua=1.

the disease that emerged

Lyle Fearnley explores how global preparedness for emerging diseases left some places unprepared.

AMONG THE VIROLOGISTS AND PUBLIC HEALTH EXPERTS WHO crafted the "emerging diseases worldview" in the 1990s, Ebola was the paradigm of an emerging disease. The Ebola virus had been discovered in 1976; it "emerged" from wildlife reservoirs in unpredictable, but dramatic and visceral outbreaks; there was no cure or vaccine.[1] Moreover, the 1989 outbreak of an Ebolavirus variant at a primate quarantine facility in Reston, Virginia—the variant, called Reston virus, was airborne but could not infect humans—led directly to the formation of the influential National Institutes of Health (NIH) and Institute of Medicine (IOM) conferences on Emerging Infections (IOM 1992; Morse 1990).[2]

With Ebola in mind, the authors of the IOM report argued that the problem of disease emergence required a novel rationality of health: preparedness for unexpected epidemics rather than the prevention, management, or eradication of already prevalent infections. At the heart of their program were recently developed surveillance technologies built on advances in computing, communication, and microbiology. Through "early warning," they suggested, new pathogens could be controlled before they spread to major population centers or threatened global pandemic (IOM 1992).

The figure of "disease emergence" helped give shape to the incipient field of global health, particularly at the World Health Organization (WHO), which restructured itself around surveillance and preparedness for emerging diseases (Brown et al. 2005; Lakoff 2010). Nongovernmental organizations also adopted the strategy: a virologist with the "virus hunting" nonprofit Metabiota summed up the hopeful mood as recently as 2012: "If we can detect it, we can stop it" (Knox 2012).

The ongoing, devastating Ebola epidemic in West Africa has revealed, however, a troubling discrepancy between the relatively early detection of an emerging disease and the very late arrival of international public health response. By March 23, 2014, less than two weeks after a health clinic in Guéckédou reported "clusters of a mysterious disease characterized by fever, severe diarrhea, vomiting, and an apparent high fatality rate" to the Guinean Ministry of Health, the Ebola virus had been isolated in European laboratories and the WHO knew there was an Ebola outbreak in Guinea (Sun et al. 2014). Some might complain that those two weeks are too long, or blame the Guéckédou clinicians who were slow to identify and report the disease because they were not trained to anticipate Ebolavirus in their community. But these lapses in reporting and identification pale in comparison to the delays in international public health intervention as the epidemic grew in full public view.

Incredibly, WHO did not declare the outbreak a "public health emergency of international concern" until August 8, more than four months after the organization was aware of the outbreak, and more than one month after Médecins San Frontières (MSF; Doctors Without Borders) declared the epidemic in Liberia was "out of control." Even more disconcerting, the declaration itself had only moderate impact: as an MSF press report from October 31 declared, the international response in Guinea remains "scattered and piecemeal."

In recent reflections, some scholars argue that the prioritization of surveillance and preparedness for emerging diseases paradoxically left West Africa vulnerable to Ebola once it emerged. Gillaume Lachenal notes that health authorities had "prepared for" the emergence of Ebola intensively, and that "pandemic preparedness exercises siphon off a large part of African health authorities' energies and resources, even as they are confronted with far more urgent health emergencies" (Lachenal 2014). Vinh-Kim Nguyen states that preparedness efforts "not only failed, they produced this Ebola epidemic" (Nguyen 2014).

Such accounts suggest that technologies of preparedness come at inherent costs to public health. They join public health scholars and practitioners who have previously criticized

---

1   On "emerging infections worldview," see King (2002).
2   The outbreak of Reston virus and its impact is documented in the popular (and influential in policy circles) journalism of Richard Preston's *The Hot Zone* (1994).

surveillance and simulation for little-known, impossible-to-predict microbes, arguing that preparedness initiatives divert attention from the fundamental social conditions and economic inequalities that truly shape the burden of disease. Global public health, these critics argue, should focus instead on the perennial and chronic afflictions (such as cholera, malaria, and HIV/AIDS) that make up the vast majority of humanity's disease burden. In this view, resources distributed for surveillance technologies or preparedness training would be better spent on basic health infrastructure, including hospital beds, trained nurses, and personal protective equipment (see, for example, Brown and Fee 2001; Farmer 2001).

The Ebola outbreak in West Africa has confirmed that an increasing capacity to detect outbreaks of emerging disease can be all too easily accompanied by the decreasing capacity to do anything about it. As Paul Farmer commented after a recent trip, "Without staff, stuff, space, and systems, nothing can be done" (Farmer 2014). Remarkably, the Metabiota "virus hunter" quoted above who spoke confidently about the importance of rapid pathogen detection (and who has been courageously working to stop the spread of Ebola in Sierra Leone) has recently pointed to the lack of basic public health infrastructure as the primary reason the epidemic remains difficult to control. "The only thing that is going to change the course of this epidemic is actual epidemiology. We need to stop the disease from being transmitted," he said in a recent interview (Weintraub 2014). But, he added, "just having the vehicles available to go do that, be they motorcycles or trucks, etc., [isn't a given]" (Weintraub 2014).

Yet to argue that preparedness for emerging diseases produced the Ebola disaster by diverting funds and attention from public health overlooks how this epidemic event undermines the simple opposition of preparedness to public health. In many

ways, the prophets of disease emergence were right: Ebola *is* a significant threat to human health, and we *should* have been preparing for it along with chronic, persistent, and already visible problems such as HIV/AIDS, cholera, and malaria. Rather than denouncing disease detection in the name of public health, I propose a more focused critique of the lack of coordination between preparedness initiatives and the infrastructure of everyday public health practice. As I have argued previously regarding "early warning" disease surveillance systems (Fearnley 2008), data collected about diseases or outbreaks are only useful if coordinated with the infrastructural scales of public health response such as hospitals, the jurisdictions of public health authority, and access to vehicles. But when it *is* so coordinated, disease surveillance for emerging diseases is a pivotal component of public health practice (Fearnley 2008).

From this perspective, the "global" preparedness programs for emerging diseases as developed to date by programs such

"Without staff, stuff, space, and systems, nothing can be done"

as the U.S. Agency for International Development (USAID's) "Emerging Pandemic Threats" program or nonprofits such as Metabiota must be critiqued in terms of their scalar logic. According to historian Nicholas King (2004), the prophets of disease emergence believed that "monitoring and intervening need not be bound to the same scale as either cause or consequence [of epidemic diseases]. Addressing 'global' risks meant making ecological change legible to laboratory investigation or information processing at multiple locations, often far removed from the specific site of disease outbreaks.(66)" Andrew Lakoff has shown that programs of "global health security," founded on an ethic of "self-protection," tend to intervene only sporadically in

BIBLIOGRAPHY

Brown, Theodore, and Elizabeth Fee. 2001. "Preemptive biopreparedness: can we learn anything from history?" *American Journal of Public Health,* 91(5): 721-726.

Brown, Theodore, Elizabeth Fee, and Marcus Cueto. 2005. "The World Health Organization and the transition from international to global public health." *American Journal of Public Health,* 95(1): 62-72.

Dehner, George. 2012. *Influenza: A century of science and public health response* Pittsburgh, PA: University of Pittsburgh Press.

Farmer, Paul. 2001. *Infections and inequalities: The modern plagues.* Berkeley: University of California.

———. 2014. "Diary." *London Review of Books,* 36(20): 38-39.

Fearnley, Lyle. 2008. "Redesigning syndromic surveillance for biosecurity." In Stephen J. Collier and Andrew Lakoff, *Biosecurity Interventions: Global Health and Security in Question,* pp. 61-88. New York: Columbia University Press.

Fidler, David. 2008. "Influenza virus samples, international law, and global health diplomacy." *Emerging Infectious Diseases,* 14(1): 88-94.

Gostin, Lawrence, and David P. Fidler. 2011. "WHO's Pandemic Influenza Preparedness Framework: A Milestone in Global Governance for Health." *Journal of the American Medical Association,* 306(2): 200-201.

Institute of Medicine (IOM). 1992. *Emerging Infections: Microbial Threats to Health.* Washington, DC: National Academies Press.

King, Nicholas. 2002. "Security, Disease, Commerce: Ideologies of Postcolonial Global Health." *Social Studies of Science,* 32(5): 763-789.

———. 2004. "The Scale Politics of Emerging Diseases." *OSIRIS,* 19: 62-76.

Knox, Richard. 2012. "Disease Detectives Catchy Deadly African Virus Just as It Emerges." *NPR,* September 17. Available at http://www.npr.org/blogs/health/2012/09/27/161912039/disease-detectives-catch-deadly-african-virus-just-as-it-emerges.

poorer countries to halt the encroachment of emerging diseases into wealthier countries (Lakoff 2010). The Ebola response has made clear the failure of this vision, both morally and in terms of technical efficacy. This failure lies not in the idea of disease surveillance or preparedness itself, but in the disregard for *linking* disease surveillance with public health and medical infrastructure, and in the neglect of their *coordination* at the same scales, locales, and jurisdictions. Such neglect can only end in disaster and, most likely, as in the current crisis, a radically unequal distribution of disaster.

What would it take to reimagine preparedness for emerging diseases in a way that also acknowledges, and attempts to ameliorate, global inequality in the access to medical and public health infrastructure? An incipient alternative may already be in formation, an outcome of the controversies about virus sharing and vaccine development during the H5N1 avian influenza outbreak. As is well known, after the emergence of the highly pathogenic H5N1 strain of influenza, the Indonesian government complained that virus samples taken from Indonesian patients and sent to WHO surveillance laboratories were subsequently given, without Indonesia's permission, to for-profit vaccine companies (Sedyaningsih 2008; compare Fidler 2008). The incident points to a broader mismeasure: since its creation in the 1940s, the WHO flu surveillance network[3] has collected viral samples from developing countries to determine the composition of the annual flu vaccine, but this vaccine was manufactured and distributed almost exclusively for populations in the developed world. Many developing countries do not have the technical or manufacturing capacity to create enough vaccines for their population, nor can they afford to purchase the requisite doses from for-profit pharmaceutical companies (Dehner 2012).

Although less immediately dramatic than the Ebola outbreak, the WHO's flu sample scandal exposes a similar lack of coordination between disease surveillance and public health response: surveillance information and biological materials go to laboratory centers in Europe or North America, but the source locales— the sites where the epidemics are taking place—do not benefit from that information. Following Indonesia's year-long campaign, the World Health Assembly ordered the WHO to restructure its surveillance system to ensure that all virus samples are accompanied by a Standard Material Transfer Agreement, which legally binds the receiving laboratory to "grant to WHO a non-exclusive, royalty-free license, which WHO will sub-license to interested developing countries, for the purpose of maximizing availability of critical benefits on a non-profit basis, such as vaccines and anti-virals, for pandemic influenza preparedness purposes" (WHO 2010; compare with Gostin and Fidler 2011).

More substantial inequalities undoubtedly are at stake in West Africa's Ebola epidemic. But Indonesia's response to the virus-sharing dispute articulates a relevant redistributive critique, not by questioning the value of surveillance and preparedness programs altogether, but rather in demanding their coordination with the scales of political authority and public health infrastructure at which epidemiological response is undertaken. Preparedness for emerging diseases can and must include preparing the vaccines, vehicles, and trained staff needed to investigate and control an epidemic *when* and *where* new diseases do emerge. ■

LYLE FEARNLEY *is Postdoctoral Fellow in Humanities, Science and Society at Nanyang Technological University, Singapore.*

---

3   Today known as the Global Influenza Surveillance Network (GISN).

Lachenal, Guillaume. 2014. "Chronicle of a Well-Prepared Disaster." *Somatosphere*, October 31. Available at http://somatosphere.net/2014/10/chronicle-of-a-well-prepared-disaster.html.

Lakoff, Andrew. 2010. "Two Regimes of Global Health." *Humanity*, 1(1):59–79.

Morse, Stephen. 1990. "Emerging Viruses: The Evolution of Viruses and Viral Diseases." *Journal of Infectious Diseases*, 162: 1–7.

Nguyen, Vinh-Kim. 2014. "How We Became Unprepared, and What Might Come Next." *Fieldsights—Hot Spots, Cultural Anthropology Online*, October 7. Available at http://www.culanth.org/fieldsights/605-ebola-how-we-became-unprepared-and-what-might-come-next.

Preston, Richard. 1994. *The Hot Zone*. New York: Random House.

Sedyaningsih, Endang R., Siti Isfandari, Triono Soendoro, and Siti Fadilah Supari. 2008. "Towards Mutual Trust, Transparency, and Equity in Virus Sharing Mechanism: The Avian Influenza Case of Indonesia." *Annals of the Academy of Medicine Singapore*, 37: 482–488.

Sun, Lena H., Brady Dennis, Lenny Bernstein, and Joel Achenbach. 2014. "How Ebola Sped Out of Control." *The Washington Post*, October 4. Available at http://www.washingtonpost.com/sf/national/2014/10/04/how-ebola-sped-out-of-control/.

Weintraub, Karen. 2014. "Q&A: American Virus Expert in Africa's Ebola Zone: 'This Is Like War'." *National Geographic*, August 8. Available at http://news.nationalgeographic.com/news/2014/08/140814-ebola-africa-america-medicine-science-world/.

World Health Organization (WHO). 2010. *Pandemic influenza preparedness: sharing of influenza viruses and access to vaccines and other benefits: Outcome of the Open-Ended Working Group of Member States on Pandemic Influenza Preparedness: sharing of influenza viruses and access to vaccines and other benefits*. Report by the Director-General, Sixty-third World Health Assembly, May 14. Available at http://apps.who.int/iris/bitstream/10665/2981/1/A63_48-en.pdf?ua=1.

Frozen By the Hot Zone

Joanna Radin explores the role of the "hot zone" in immobilizing people, blood and information.

EBOLA'S ABILITY TO TRAVEL HAS BEEN WELL PUBLICIZED, but there is another story: one of immobility. In West Africa, research materials that contribute to improving knowledge about the disease such as blood samples and patient records have been trapped or entangled in the "hot zone." In some circumstances, the virulence of such materials appears to pose a risk to biosecurity that may be greater than their ability to help mitigate that risk. In times of uncertainty, fear may trump established policies about how to manage the flow of people, information, and research materials. For instance, while the World Health Organization (WHO) has been opposed to travel restrictions to ensure continued circulation of health workers, the home institutions that employ such workers may choose to impose such restrictions. In such cases, prevention is seen as a preferable alternative to quarantine should health workers return with infection. Yet, physicians and health workers who have been able to travel between makeshift treatment camps in Africa and the resource-rich laboratories and medical centers in the Global North

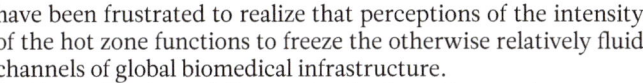

have been frustrated to realize that perceptions of the intensity of the hot zone functions to freeze the otherwise relatively fluid channels of global biomedical infrastructure.

Since the time of Pasteur in the late nineteenth century, blood, tissue, urine, and stool samples collected at the sites of epidemics have been crucial resources for increasing knowledge about infectious disease (Anderson 2010; Neill 2012). With the rise of cryopreservation in the decades after World War II, blood samples could be accumulated and shipped to biomedical laboratories for analysis (Radin 2014). Often these samples would travel in coolers or liquid nitrogen Dewar flasks held on the laps of researchers as they flew back from the field. Today, the biospecimen—both cryopreserved as well as freshly collected—continues

from patient to health care provider. Ease of movement in personal protective equipment (PPE) is an acquired skill. It is not something that can be learned in 20 minutes. PPE also hampers existing skills. One cannot listen to lungs or put in an IV easily while wearing the so-called "moon suits." In the tropical climates of Western Africa, a health worker can only perform a short stint in such gear before taking a break to hydrate.

In such circumstances, the medical chart becomes an important means of sharing information between health workers who are rapidly cycling on and off shifts. Jacquerioz explained that keeping track of fluid loss, which is so extreme in Ebola patients that it often comes to be measured by buckets, is an essential component of care. However, since paper medical charts often are splattered with droplets of bodily substance in the course of care, they can quickly become classified as a biohazard. This means that it is not easy for medical records to travel beyond the clinic.

Patient information has been making it out of the hot zone through health care workers' use of the cameras on their smartphones. Taking pictures of the records is emerging as a makeshift workaround, but may not lead to data aggregation for analysis. The idea that "big data" could be used to combat Ebola is undermined by the fact that there is not enough data; the data that matter are still hard to get (Wall 2014). Most of the big data claims are based on reports of suspected or actual cases by those who hear about or observe symptoms of infection. They have not been based on the kind of validated patient and genomic information we might assume is at the heart of medical big data, in part because obtaining that data is incredibly difficult both technically and bureaucratically.

Richard Preston, author of the 1990s technothriller *The Hot Zone*, recently wrote in the *New Yorker* about how hard it has

The real heroes [of the West African epidemic] are the people who cannot or do not leave.

to be an invaluable resource for learning about emerging infections diseases. Yet, the perceived virulence of Ebola, the great uncertainty about its mechanisms, and the resource challenges that undermine efforts to adhere to best practices has made it extremely difficult to traffic in blood. It has made it hard to move biospecimens at all, despite the existence of special protocols for doing so (WHO 2014).

In November of 2014, for instance, Frederique Jacquerioz, a physician and researcher based at Tulane University Medical School, presented a dispatch at the American Society of Tropical Medicine and Hygiene (ASTMH) annual meeting in New Orleans titled "From the Hot Zone: A Clinician's Perspective on Confronting Ebola Virus in West Africa." She had been in Liberia several months earlier and described the challenges to treatment and knowledge production presented by the logic of containment.

These challenges begin with the protective gear that is considered be most effective in reducing transmission of Ebola virus

been to circulate Ebola blood samples (Preston 2014). While some blood made it out of Sierra Leone in May, "[a] thousand more vials of human blood with Ebola in them are sitting in freezers in Kenema waiting for bureaucratic clearance so that they can be flown to Harvard and sequenced in the machines, and scientists can see what the swarm has been doing more recently" (Preston 2014).

Other high-tech interventions have shown their limits in West African contexts. The point of care test device known as POC-T, developed for use in the emergency rooms of Euro-American hospitals, has been adopted as a way of quickly obtaining vital statistics in the hot zone. But because it is hot in terms of temperature as well as virulence, these devices frequently overheat and fail. Jacquerioz reported that she and her peers had to take time to use ice that was already in short supply to cool the devices so function could be restored.

It is not only research materials and data that have been frozen in place. In the Q & A session following Jacquerioz's presentation at ASTMH, a researcher and physician who identified himself as having "named the bloody thing" in the 1970s raised the question of nursing care. He asked whether or not those who had seroconverted and survived Ebola were being enrolled as frontline support in caring for patients in the hot zone. The answer is yes. Jacquerioz emphasized that right now, "the real heroes [of the West African epidemic] are the people who cannot or do not leave."

Beyond those international health care workers who choose to remain in the hot zone, a recent article in *Wired* magazine highlights the complex social role of individuals whose agency is more mediated; those who have survived and stayed to perform caring labor. "All their possessions are gone, destroyed while they were sick to avoid contamination. They feel shunned, even as they work to save others" (Hayden 2014). Recovery in such a situation has become situated as a biological and social imperative to remain at the epicenter of suffering. The international public health community may view nurses in places such as Sierra Leone as heroes, but their return to the hot zone is also a result of the stigma they experience by having been ill. Inadequacies in health infrastructure and fear about the spread of infection that make it difficult for biospecimens and patient information to circulate also contribute to the circumstances that make it difficult for survivors to move on.

Even those who can leave the hot zone have found that the stigma of having been exposed to Ebola constrains their ability to participate in efforts to share knowledge about the epidemic.

At the ASTMH—among the most important gatherings in the field of infectious disease—the Louisiana Department of Health and Hospitals attempted to impose quarantine restrictions on researchers traveling to the meeting from any of three Ebola-affected countries (Governor's Office of Homeland Security and Disaster Preparedness 2014). Prospective meeting participants were greeted with the threat of isolation:

Welcome to New Orleans

① *Within the past 21 days, have you traveled from Liberia, Sierra Leone, or Guinea?*
② *Do you have flu-like symptoms and a fever?*
③ *Have you been exposed to someone who was suspected or known to have Ebola?*

If you answered YES to questions ① or ③, please call our 24-Hour hotline...

As the epidemic continues to unfold and public health officials continue to make decisions based on partial information and with inadequate resources, people (survivors) and things (medical charts, blood samples) are being both produced and contained by the hot zone. Getting anything or anyone out of the hot zone, even a recovered patient or healthy researcher, has become a chilling dimension of this epidemic. ∎

JONNA RADIN *is an Assistant Professor in the Section for the History of Medicine at Yale University, where she is also a member of the Program for History of Science and Medicine and the Departments of History and of Anthropology.*

BIBLIOGRAPHY

Anderson, Warwick. 2010. "Crap on the Map, or Postcolonial Waste." *Postcolonial Studies* 13(2): 169-187.

Governor's Office of Homeland Security and Disaster Preparedness. 2014. "Louisiana Ebola Virus Disease Response Plan." October 30. Available at http://gohsep.la.gov/plans/2014_Louisiana_Ebola_Response_Plan_Annex.pdf.

Hayden, Erika Check. 2014. "In Sierra Leone, Nurses Who Survive Ebola Return to Help Others." *Wired*, Dec 8, Available at: http://www.wired.com/2014/12/sierra-leone-nurses-survive-ebola-return-to-help/

Neill, Deborah J. 2012. *Networks in Tropical Medicine: Internationalism, Colonialism, and the Rise of a Medical Specialty.* Stanford, CA: Stanford University Press.

Preston, Richard. 2014. "The Ebola Wars." *The New Yorker*, Oct. 27, 2014, Available at: http://www.newyorker.com/magazine/2014/10/27/ebola-wars.

Radin, Joanna. 2014. "Unfolding Epidemiological Stories: How the WHO Made Frozen Blood into a Flexible Resource for the Future." *Studies in History and Philosophy of Biological and Biomedical Sciences,* 47: 62-73.

Wall, Matthew. 2014. "Ebola: Can Big Data Analytics Help Contain Its Spread?" *BBC News*, October 14. Available at http://www.bbc.com/news/business-29617831.

World Health Organization (WHO). 2014. " Laboratory Guidance for the Diagnosis of Ebola Virus Disease: Interim Recommendations." September 19. Available at http://apps.who.int/iris/bitstream/10665/134009/1/WHO_EVD_GUIDANCE_LAB_14.1_eng.pdf.

What does experimentation look like in the time of emergency?

ebola, running ahead

Ann H. Kelly explores the design of clinical trials amidst the ebola crisis.

"Our response was too orientated toward the management of previous outbreaks," explained Jean-Hervé Bradol, the director of Médecins Sans Frontières' (MSF; Doctors Without Borders) internal review body, the Centre de Réflexion sur l'Action et les Savoirs Humanitaires (CRASH). "We wasted time before speaking about a vaccine and treatments. It's very hard to imagine controlling this epidemic now without a vaccine" (Flynn and Bartunek 2014).

In an outbreak, public health is haunted by the specter of belatedness. Delays in diagnosis reduce survival rates; sluggish case-detection redoubles contagion. Time's ravages are materialized by a single equation: the reproductive ratio, or R_0, which determines the average number of people a sick individual will infect. Spreading only through close physical contact with very sick people or corpses, Ebola's R_0 is not of an apocalyptic order. Its virulence, while terrifying, is ultimately self-limiting, as patients routinely die before they can infect many others. Reducing transmission is thus relatively straightforward: the sick must be isolated, their contacts monitored, and the dead safely buried. In the 24 known outbreaks recorded since the virus was first identified in 1976, these approaches have kept the numbers of infected lower than 200 on average.

Needless to say, the current situation in West Africa is different. A year now from the first or "index" case, the disease has "ping-ponged" from village to city and back, moving into new districts, spilling across borders, and boarding planes. The reasons for this outbreak's magnitude—approaching 18,000 cases and well over 6,000 reported deaths (as of early December 2014)—are both structural and contingent: the density and mobility of the population; an endemic distrust of the government; perilously weak health systems; the underfunding of the World Health Organization (WHO) and an excessive reliance on MSF; the death of a high-profile imam; the siting of a treatment center; the decision to not give a well-known local doctor access to experimental treatment, etc. Whatever the reason, the outbreak's pace is now a feature of its own scale. Dragging the R_0 down will demand population-level methods.

Protective span is vaccine territory, and there are currently several candidates in the pipeline, two of which are in advanced stages of development. GlaxoSmithKline's

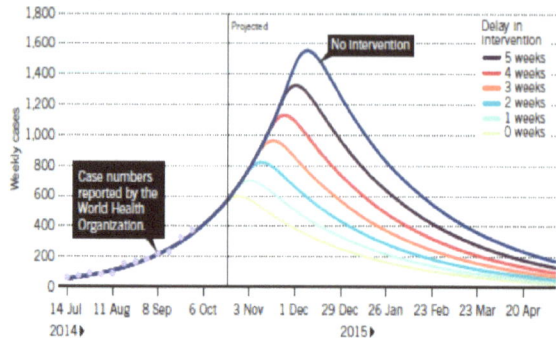

DELAYS MEAN MORE DEATHS
For every week that effective interventions are not implemented in Ebola-stricken areas, the case-number peak will be pushed higher and later, meaning that more hospital beds will be needed.

FIGURE 1 "Behind the curve" of contagion.

(GSK) cAd3-ZEBO vaccine, involving a non-replicating chimpanzee adenovirus, has been shown to be safe in healthy volunteers and is on track for large-scale clinical trials among afflicted populations as early as January 2015. An alternative vaccine, rVSV-ZEBO, developed by the Canadian company NewLink Genetics in collaboration with Merck and based on a weakened version of the vesicular stomatitis virus (VSV), is not far behind. While the details of trial design, locations, and target populations are still being worked out, these investigations will be supported by MSF, which will provide trial locations, funding, and clinical oversight.[1]

The paradigmatic example of biomedical triumphalism, a successful vaccine offers the promise of a way of tackling the current outbreak and a permanent solution for those yet to come (compare Rees 2014). But while expectations are high, immunization is not the only method on trial. In a seeming radical reversal of protocol, MSF and other international and nongovernmental aid organizations are emphasizing community-based responses, involving the distribution of home disinfection kits and the construction of Ebola care units staffed by non-expert volunteers.

What MSF describes as "unprecedented and imperfect measures" clearly belong to a different "political economy of hope" than the Ebola-free futures projected by the

---

1   cAd3 is a chimpanzee adenovirus which is nonpathogenic in humans. Complemented with a gene that codes for the glycoproteins of a Zaire Ebola strain, cAd3 provokes an immune response to Ebola virus. The vesicular stomatitis virus (VSV) is a pathogen found in livestock, and is similarly engineered to carry a gene from the Zaire ebolavirus. Single doses of both vaccines have shown 100% protection in nonhuman primates at 4 to 5 weeks and promising immune response in humans. In contrast to cAd3, however, VSV replicates for 2 to 3 days within humans, which induces a stronger immune response to Ebola and may offer longer protection. Studies of the immune response and safety of using cAd3 with a booster, MVA-BN Filo, designed by the Danish pharmaceutical company Bavarian Nordic are currently under way at the University of Oxford.

2   A target which Liberia and Guinea have met but Sierra Leone has not (UNMEER situation report, December 8, 2014).

cAd3-ZEBO and VSV-ZEBO vaccines (MSF 2014; Novas 2006). And yet, vaccines and community-based methods share an impetus to re-create the temporality of control, to restore a "response time" that seems increasingly out of joint. "Going forward we are now hunting the virus, chasing after the virus," said WHO Director-General Margaret Chan said in a recent interview (Mazumdar 2014). As long as the outbreak is able to "run ahead" of efforts to contain it, she noted, the "risk to the world is always there" (Mazumdar 2014). Through a series of compromises and hedges between care and experimentation, a complex technical assemblage of humanitarian biomedicine is now in operation, an assemblage that attempts to simultaneously address individual survival and global security (Lakoff 2010; Redfield 2012).

PRE-PRESENTATION

A quick "burnout" was what MSF—de facto the only organization capable of managing viral hemorrhagic outbreaks—had expected. But when Ebola cropped up in cities—Conakry (Guinea), Monrovia (Liberia), and finally Freetown (Sierra Leone)—tracking and isolating individual cases became impossible. Well-equipped and expert-staffed treatment centers were overwhelmed and, in some cases, functioned only as spaces of quarantine. Those who sought treatment traveled further in search of quality care, potentially infecting others along the way. Many others came to associate clinics with death and chose to stay at home, avoiding contact with health services altogether.

When the international response finally kicked into gear it established an ambitious benchmark: isolating 70% of cases by December 1, 2014, and 100% by the beginning of 2015.[2] To that end, foreign governments pledged human and material resources to build and staff new centers. From the start, however, these efforts were caught in a game of catch-up, chasing exponential projections that placed the number of beds perpetually behind the curve (Figure 1).

Again, the issue here is timing. It is not enough to isolate patients: they must be secluded before they are infective (within three days of the first symptoms, the models suggest). Slowing transmission thus demands expanding the biomedical frontier from centers of expertise to the uncertain realm of the "community."

Community Care Units (CCUs) provide that extension. Drawing on a concept of "community care" originally developed within the UK National Health Service in the 1960s (Draper 1967), Ebola CCUs are now being erected in the outskirts of villages and periurban neighborhoods all across the outbreak area, using tents, tarps, makeshift materials, and repurposed buildings. CCUs can provide anywhere from 10 to 30 beds and are supported by unspecialized and minimally trained volunteers from the community—ideally survivors—using equipment and supplies donated by humanitarian agencies. Clean water, sanitation, and food and basic medicine are provided; care is primarily palliative. Diagnosis or any other interventions that requires drawing blood is not among the services offered. Because Ebola's early-stage symptoms are considered relatively less serious, a single health worker is expected to manage several patients at a time.

The number of CCUs has grown rapidly; the UK government plans to build at least 200 more. Guidelines are still being hammered out. As Chris Whitty and colleagues put it, "optimal design will be learned on the fly. We know how to minimize infection in dedicated Ebola wards with highly trained and supervised staff, but not in facilities with lightly trained staff in which most people do not have Ebola (but some do)" (2014:194).

While uncertainties remain regarding the quality of care and the risks involved in its delivery, CCUs are not conceived as ends in themselves, but rather as instruments of triage: a waiting post until patients whose cases are confirmed can be sent to a proper treatment facility. Within this framework, even the distribution of personal protective equipment to households is not seen as a last-ditch humanitarian effort, but rather as another link in a chain that will eventually lead one to the expert care provided by MSF (Leach et al. 2014).

The key selling point of the CCU is its proximity to the community, in space and in spirit. If this outbreak has taught us anything, it is that disease control is not merely a question of access but also of acceptability; until quite recently, the response has been perilously short on both. By enfolding the grassroots into health care delivery, the CCU provides a stopgap to containment efforts, but only if patients regard these places as sites where they will receive quality care. Things will fall part, as one MSF logistician put it, "if people feel that they are being left with scraps, while Europeans are treated with ZMAPP."

In short, CCUs operate under the expectation that biomedical resources—in the form of cures, diagnostics, staff, and support—are at hand. Of course, with no drug or vaccine yet available and with a patient fatality rate around 60%, the promise of care feels shallow. "Given the risks that health workers take, getting Ebola vaccines to staff working in the units as soon as they have proved safe is an ethical imperative" (Whitty et al. 2014:194).

SPEEDING VACCINES

Incredibly, that time might not be far off. International consortia involving academic, government, and commercial partners have been quickly assembled to design and implement fast-track clinical trials; regulatory requirements have been streamlined; plans have been put forward to set up an indemnity fund to insure pharmaceutical companies if the vaccines prove to have any dangerous side effects, and the United States has provided immunity against any legal claims (Federal Register 2014). Having shrunk the timeline from the usual years to months, preparations have begun for large-scale studies in Ebola-affected countries to begin in January 2015.

While logistical questions remain—ranging from the number of doses needed to the cold-chain requirements for vaccine delivery—the most pressing concern is which population to target. Prioritizing "frontline workers"—those clinicians, contact tracers, burial teams, and volunteers providing community-based care—is the obvious strategy: in addition to being at greater risk of infection, these groups are arguably more capable of understanding the risks of an experimental vaccine. Informed consent, it is reasoned, will be more genuine and the potential back-lash vaccines often create—for example, rumors about sterilization—will be minimized (e.g. Feldman-Savelsberg et al. 2000; Kaler 2009). Whether or not foreign health volunteers should be included in that cohort is unclear.

Another possibility being considered is a "ring vaccination" approach, like the one used during the WHO campaign to eradicate smallpox. This involves containing new foci of infection, targeting primary or secondary contacts of the infected, and following the importation of the disease to new countries. While the data suggest that while the fatality rate is much higher for those over the age of 45, it is likely that people will want their children were prioritized for vaccination.

In any case, selecting inclusion criteria is not merely a matter of determining who would benefit the most if the vaccine should prove successful. The explicit motivation for accelerating development is that a vaccine can address *this* outbreak. MSF's Jean-Hervé Bradol's admonitions express a frustration: if clinical trials had started earlier, transmission could have been halted and lives saved.

But regardless of the impact a vaccine would have on transmission ongoing in West Africa, the outbreak offers a scientific opportunity. "This must be the last time we are taken by surprise" was a refrain at the WHO Ebola Vaccine Consultation back in September. A vaccine has the unique capacity to act as bulwark against the unforeseen. Indeed, while the industry has capacity to produce vaccines in bulk, by the time trials are concluded, the dent a large-scale immunization program would make in the current West Africa epidemic would be relatively small. Rather, development is driven by the "inevitability" of future outbreaks: "All efforts to develop, test, and approve vaccines must be followed through to completion at the current accelerated pace...as a contribution to global health security, fully licensed and approved vaccines should be stockpiled in readiness for the next Ebola outbreak" (WHO 2014).

For pharmaceutical companies, government stockpiles would certainly mitigate the financial risks of developing a drug for which the poor cannot pay. However, to achieve this goal, companies must be sure that they have clear indications of vaccine efficacy. It is still unclear, for instance, how acceleration will affect the quality of the data required for licensure; the position of the U.S. Federal Drug Administration (FDA) on the evaluation of these "fast-track" trials is still open.

It is precisely at this point where the humanitarian and biosecurity potentials of the vaccine come into conflict. The FDA has so far been emphatic that randomized, double-blinded, placebo-controlled clinical trials (RCTs) are necessary for licensure. MSF, however, has put up strong

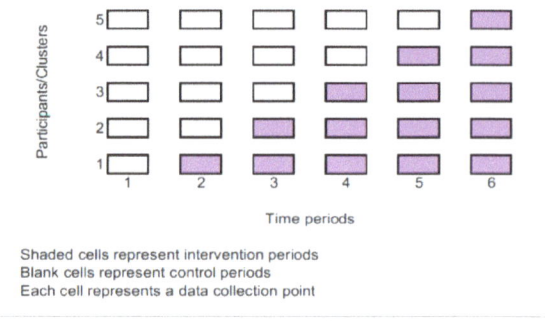

FIGURE 2 Example of a stepped wedge study design.
SOURCE: BROWN AND LILFORD 2006

opposition to a trial design that would mean denying potentially effective protection to those most at risk. While arguably there is genuine uncertainty about the benefits of these vaccines, the promise of the early-stage studies and the scale of the current outbreak have pitted concerns about investigative rigor against ethical imperatives of equity and compassion. The political consequences of these experiments are further amplified by fraught histories of mass immunization and iatrogenesis in Africa (e.g., Lachenal et al. 2010; Feldman-Savelsberg et al. 2000; Moulin 1996). As Eric Karikari Boateng, the head of the Laboratory Services Department at the Ghanaian Food and Drugs Authority, put it: "For the African community we must have high quality protection that satisfies international standards, not rushed African standards (WHO, Consultation September 28th, 2014)."[3]

To enact this balance between investigative integrity and humanitarian compassion, between accelerated access and unnecessary exposure, a few strategies are being pursued. First, RCTs of safety and immunogenicity will take place among Africa populations in "at-risk settings," but not where there is currently high transmission: for instance, Mali, Cameroon, or Ghana. These investigations will generate data on dosage and safety, adverse reactions, and reactivity with HIV/AIDS or other compromising infections. Almost simultaneously, head-to-head vaccine trials, comparing the two candidates potentially with a booster, will be rolled out in affected populations using an adapted randomized schedule referred to as a "stepped wedge" design (Figure 2). This will involve vaccinating groups in a sequence over an extended period of time (probably about a month): everyone will get vaccinated, but some before others. A stepped wedge has previously been used in situations where the intervention on trial is believed to do more good than harm or, alternatively, where logistical reasons (e.g., a limited supply) makes a simultaneous roll-out of the intervention to all participants difficult (compare Halloran 2010). Such a design presents obvious challenges, however, as the lag time might introduce new bias. What if virus mutates, for instance, or the incidence of other diseases (such as malaria) rises and interferes with the vaccine's immunological response? Yet staggering the intervention into steps provides an opportunity to stop the trial if the vaccine proves

---

3   These discussions are overshadowed by the memory of scandalous HIV research: most infamously, the short-course AZT trials conducted across Africa in the mid-1990s, whereby treatment known to prevent mother-to-child transmission of HIV/AIDS was compared with a placebo (compare Angell 1997). Thus, while the case was made for rapid, clear, and contextually relevant results, the clear commercial advantages of structural inequities have complicated these positions (Petryna 2005).

to be ineffective. It creates the space to experiment within an emergency, to balance countervailing norms of access and evidence.

Protocols are still being finalized; the questions these experiments raise are legion. At the WHO back in September, Dr. Nicole Lurie, the Assistant Secretary for Preparedness and Response in the U.S. Department of Health and Human Services (HHS) emphasized that "time is not on our side." Quick decisions had to be made about the dosage level and the inclusion of vulnerable populations (e.g., patients with HIV, pregnant women) in a situation where very little is known about what immune response will be good enough to ensure protection. Experimental vaccines and therapies should be made available but without any clear sense of their efficacy.

Would populations storm experimental sites or run from them in fear? "This is a Kafkaesque situation," Dr. Lurie conceded. It seemed a perfect epithet for the compulsion and deferral that characterizes humanitarian experimentation. ∎

ANN H. KELLY is Senior Lecturer in Anthropology in the Department of Sociology, Philosophy, and Anthropology at the University of Exeter. Her work focuses on the practices of medical research and scientific production, with special attention to the built environment, material artefacts, and practical labors of experimentation in sub-Saharan Africa. From April 2016, she will be Senior Lecturer in Global Health in the Department of Social Science, Health & Medicine, at Kings College London.

BIBLIOGRAPHY

Angell, Marcia. 1997. "The Ethics of Clinical Research in the Third World." *New England Journal of Medicine*, 337(12): 847–849.

Brown, Celia A., and Richard J. Lilford. 2006. "The Stepped Wedge Trial Design: A Systematic Review." *BMC Medical Research Methodology*, 6(54):*PMC*. Web. 15 Dec. 2014. doi:10.1186/1471-2288-6-54. Available at: http://www.biomedcentral.com/1471-2288/6/54

Draper, Peter. 1967. "Community-care Units and Inpatient Units as Alternatives to the District General Hospital." *The Lancet*, 290(7531):1406–1409.

Federal Register. 2014. "Notice Of Declaration Under The Public Readiness And Emergency Preparedness Act." December 10. Available at https://www.federalregister.gov/articles/2014/12/10/2014-28856/ebola-virus-disease-vaccines.

Feldman-Savelsberg Pamela, Flavien T. Ndonko, and Bergis. Schmidt-Ehry. 2000. "Sterilizing Vaccines or the Politics of the Womb: Retrospective Study of a Rumor in the Cameroon." *Medical Anthropology Quarterly*, 14:159–179.

Flynn, Daniel, and Robert-Jan Bartunek. 2014. "Exclusive: MSF Should Have Called for Ebola Vaccine Earlier, Says Aid Group Veteran." *Reuters*, Nov. 14. Available at http://www. reuters.com/article/2014/11/14/us-health-ebola-msfidUSKCN0IY0CI20141114.

Halloran, M. Elizabeth, Ira M. Longini Jr, and Claudio J. Struchiner, et al. 2010. *Design and Analysis of Vaccine Studies*. New York: Springer.

et al. Lachenal, Guillaume, Preston Marx, William Schneider, Ernest Drucker, and François Simon. 2010. "Simian Viruses and Emerging Diseases in Human Beings." *The Lancet*, 376(9756):1901–1902.

Kaler, Amy. 2009. "Health interventions and the persistence of rumour: the circulation of sterility stories in African public health campaigns." *Social science & medicine* 68 (9): 1711–1719.

Lakoff, Andrew. 2010. "Two Regimes of Global Health." *Humanity: An International Journal of Human Rights, Humanitarianism, and Development*, 1(1):59–79.

Leach, Melissa, Fred Martineau, and Pauline Oosterhoff. 2014. "Increasing Early Presentation to ECU Through Improving Care." *Anthropology Ebola Response Platform Policy Brief*. Available at http://www.ebola-anthropology.net/wp/content/uploads/2014/11/Increasing-early-presentation-to-ECUthrough-improving-care.pdf.

Mazumdar, Tulip. 2014. "Ebola Outbreak: Virus Still 'Running Ahead of Us,' says WHO." *BBC News*, December 10. Available at http://www.bbc.co.uk/news/health-30400304.

Médecins Sans Frontières (MSF). 2014. "Ebola: Massive Distribution of Home Disinfection Kits Underway in Monrovia." October 2. Available at http://www.doctorswithoutborders.org/news-stories/field-news/ebola-massive-distribution-home-disinfection-kits-underway-monrovia.

Moulin, Anne-Marie 1996. *L'Aventure de la vaccination*. Fayard: Paris.

Novas, Carlos. 2006. "The Political Economy of Hope: Patient's Organizations, Science and Biovalue." *BioSocieties*, 1:289–305.

Petryna, Adriana. 2005. "Ethical Variability: Drug Development and Globalizing Clinical Trials. *American Ethnologist*, 32(2):183–197.

Redfield, Peter. 2102. "Bioexpectations: Life Technologies as Humanitarian Goods." *Public Culture*, 24.1(66):157–184.

Rees, Tobias. 2014. "Humanity/plan; or, on the 'Stateless' Today (also Being an Anthropology of Global Health)." *Cultural Anthropology*, 29(3):457–478.

World Health Organization (WHO). 2014. "WHO High-level Meeting on Ebola Vaccines Access and Financing." Summary Report, October 23. Available at http://apps.who.int/iris/bitstream/10665/137184/1/WHO_EVD_Meet_EMP_14.2_eng.pdf.

Where There Is No Kit

Where there is no kit and no infrastructure, there is vulnerability. Peter Redfield explores the role of medical humanitarian response in the Ebola crisis.

AT LONG LAST, DOOMSDAY HAS ARRIVED. Ebola's Atlantic passage may have mixed genres of tragedy and farce—real human suffering and cable news—but finally a sense of urgency matches years of apocalyptic prophecy. We were prepared, until we were not. And now the emergency is indeed upon us (Lachenal 2014; Nguyen 2014; see also Caduff 2014; Lakoff 2014).

I approach this crisis moment after years of following one group cast in a leading role: Médecins Sans Frontières (MSF; Doctors Without Borders).[1] As a private, medical organization with global humanitarian ambitions, MSF is paradoxically both technically well-primed and constitutionally ill-suited to take the lead with such an outbreak. On the one hand it possesses a well-developed set of protocols and a logistics system designed for emergency response. On the other hand it operates as independently as possible, engages on multiple fronts worldwide and issues moral exhortations, not commands. Like an emergency physician, MSF primarily seeks to stabilize patients, deferring responsibility for their future well-being to existing authorities. The current outbreak, however, reveals the full extent to which this approach presumes the existence of political, as well as technical health infrastructure.

From the perspective of medical humanitarianism, Ebola appears a relatively exotic problem: deadly and disturbingly unknown, but also thankfully rare and usually delimited in its geographic scope. Relative to such common concerns as malaria, malnutrition, and AIDS, it affects comparatively few people, and only in episodic flashes. Even cholera, a classic epidemic disease, appears with depressing consistency around the world when people find themselves displaced, and thus plays a far more significant role in humanitarian portfolio. In 2013 (a low year), MSF treated 27,900 patients with cholera, many times the total number who had ever experienced Ebola in the past, and still more than official numbers for the current outbreak. Indeed, the regular appearance of cholera helped inspire the group's logistics system, built around standard kits of prepackaged materials stored in anticipation of emergencies worldwide. In the case of cholera, the kit system generally succeeds in saving lives. A rapid, prepackaged response of public health sanitation usually eradicates the immediate epidemic, if not, sadly, its root causes.

Despite the relative rarity of Ebola, MSF developed a measure of familiarity with the condition after responding to a series of African outbreaks over the last two decades. Along with the World Health Organization (WHO) and the U.S. Centers for Disease control (CDC), the group can even claim a certain expertise with the disease. It is important to note that this expertise derives from internal initiative, not any formal mandate. If not a major threat in statistical terms, Ebola did appear in exactly the settings where humanitarians frequently found themselves: largely rural landscapes in countries such as Democratic Republic of Congo, Gabon, and Uganda. This was MSF's home turf, so to speak, as much or more than any other medical entity. Thus, by the turn of the millennium, the organization also had developed a kit for Ebola—or rather a set of three kits—described in a briefing document from November 2001 (Baert 2001:65).[2] In addition to a standard package shipped from Belgium in seven modules, including a full complement of medical and protective supplies, the document outlines two smaller configurations, one designed for initial assessment of potential outbreaks and another for local health centers. With regard to the latter, its author emphasizes the need for proper training, without which the equipment might provide only a false sense of security.

Ebola, after all, remains unnervingly at the edge of medical capacity. Here it is important to distinguish between the protection of public health and the provision of clinical care. Until now, intervention has focused on setting up a quarantined treatment center in an effort to arrest the spread of disease and safeguard the surrounding population. All previous Ebola responses ultimately achieved this goal of preventing future infections. For existing patients who arrive at one of these centers, however, the treatment has been distressingly minimal: medical staff endeavor to provide basic supportive care (rehydrating, maintaining oxygen status and blood pressure, treating any complicating infections) and essentially hope that the patient recovers. The uncomfortable fact is that they have had little more to offer, however well trained they might be. Although varying by viral strain and treatment context, the disease has unnervingly high death rates, often higher than 50% and running as high as 90% (CDC 2014). Moreover, while Ebola may not be especially infectious as far as viruses go, the manner in which it disrupts a host body—multiplying as the patient declines and increasingly oozing out in bodily fluids—places caregivers at particular risk. Both treating an infected person and tending to a corpse become hazardous acts. Indeed, care itself becomes a primary vector of transmission. As a consequence, Ebola eats through the very bonds of human compassion, infecting those who offer assistance: relatives, mourners, and health care professionals.

Due to this heightened risk of transmission, medical personnel themselves feel acutely vulnerable. They don an elaborate second skin of protective equipment before attending to Ebola patients. Once done with a shift they shed this shell, laboriously adhering to strict protocols and nervously hoping to avoid exposure. Commentators often note that the outfit strongly resembles a space suit, and similarly signals a primary need for self-preservation.[3] Seeking to seal themselves from the hostile environment of their patients, caregivers effectively become

---

1   For current information on MSF, see the international site at www.msf. org and the U.S. site at http://www.doctorswithoutborders.org. See also the MSF Ebola blog page at http://blogs.msf.org/en/staff/blogs/msf-ebola-blog. For recent profiles of the organization, see Redfield (2013) and Fox (2014).

2   See also http://www.medbox.org/ebola-outbreak-preparedness-management/preview?q=baert
3   The connection to space contains a historical thread, since early astronauts underwent precautionary quarantine in a converted trailer following their return from the moon: http://life.time.com/history/ebola-vs-apollo-11-quarantine-after-splashdown/#1. This thread in turn loops back to the genre of outbreak thrillers, setting the script for later nonfiction writing: http://www.thecrimson.com/article/1969/8/12/infectious-pbtbhe-andromeda-strain-by-michael/. See also Wald 2008.

otherworldly figures, frightening as well as frightened. As widely reported earlier in this exceptional West African outbreak, Ebola teams can incite suspicion and arouse resistance. The appearance of ghostly aliens who keep patients at arms' length, spray everything with disinfectant, and then hurriedly spirit them away to a distant location where they often die does little to inspire confidence. Staff from several organizations, including MSF, found their vehicles pelted with rocks, and members of a Guinean education team were murdered (Wilson 2014).

Such extreme distrust and violence becomes less surprising in light of the longer history of the disease. Earlier responses to outbreaks likewise provoked a swirl of rumors, active mistrust, and attempted flight by patients (Hewlett and Hewlett 2008:56–57; see also McCoy 2014). They also inspired misgivings and soul-searching on the part of caregivers. A report from a 2001 workshop on "Justice and MSF Operational Choices" addressed the Ugandan outbreak of the previous year at some length. It noted that while MSF had been invited to help on the basis of its clinical experience to reduce hospital infections, the very practice of aggregating patients together might have had the opposite effect:

> The public health response was probably being dealt with in the traditional (local) way by shutting people away in the barn and not feeding them or looking after them. Such a response traditionally would probably have broken the epidemic as quickly as anything we did, but the motivation for MSF was the alleviation of individual suffering. Alleviation of suffering and dying with dignity was enormously important. We know we saved very few lives (MSF-Holland 2001:26).

Whether or not the report accurately represents local response, it does recognize the possibility of iatrogenic harm, a somber possibility that extended beyond care itself.[4] Even the group's desire to reduce stigma related to the disease had encountered an unexpected obstacle in overexposure, as "we felt that the world-wide publicity probably made things look worse" (MSF-Holland 2001:26).

If not saving that many lives, then what did MSF's response achieve? Did the supportive care at least have palliative effects, easing suffering and allowing patients to die with dignity? At an annual meeting of MSF-France in 2005, debate surfaced about recent treatment of Marburg virus (closely related to Ebola) in Angola. As recounted in the section's internal newsletter:

> A member of the audience described that we were reduced to "health police", while another expressed regret concerning the remote, paranoiac attitude of the majority of caregivers, increasing the gap already exists between doctor and patient. Most ultimately agreed that the brutality of the operation was regrettable, and concluded that in future anthropologists and psychologists should be involved to a greater degree in such circumstances, since caregivers' actions consist here in particular of supporting the patients and their loved ones through the dying process (MSF 2005:14).

In later operations, MSF would attempt to some degree to recognize the humanity of its patients. A 2008 edition of MSF guidelines calls for efforts to demystify Ebola treatment centers by allowing people to see inside them, as well as providing survivors and relatives of the deceased with a "solidarity kit" to compensate them for items destroyed for fear of contamination (Sterk 2008). And, as reported in academic and nonacademic media, both WHO and MSF have belatedly recognized a role for anthropologists in navigating responses (Hewlett and Hewlett 2008; Sáez et al. 2014). Yet all proved too little, too late for the current outbreak. When the virus unexpectedly appeared in West Africa, humanity took a backseat to security. The breach in the larger social membrane, however, ran deeper and wider than any gap in protective clothing (Frankfurter 2014).

> ## Ebola, after all, remains unnervingly at the edge of medical capacity.

As the disease escaped initial containment, panic began to set in. Protocols, kits, and hasty attempts at quarantine could not substitute for incapacity, poor judgment, and early inaction. In some settings (Senegal, Democratic Republic of Congo and—to great relief—Nigeria), public health efforts managed to smother local outbreaks, erasing them from the headlines. In others, however, disaster only grew. After initial eruption in Guinea, the patchwork, aid-based circulatory system of medical care in Liberia and Sierra Leone dissolved before the onslaught, itself endangering a much broader pool of patients (MSF 2014h). From the outset, MSF was working on the front lines. The organization's own news briefs, initially measured and businesslike, began to express alarm by the end of March, recognizing the geographic dispersal of cases was unprecedented; then, when hope of containment failed, it pronounced the epidemic out of control by mid-June (MSF 2014d; see also MSF 2014g; Wieners and Kitamura 2014).[5] The updates grew increasingly shrill as the summer wore on and conditions deteriorated. In early September, feeling overwhelmed, the group took the extraordinary step of calling for military support (though not forced quarantine). In a speech to the United Nations, MSF's international president Dr. Joanne Liu accused member states of joining a "global coalition of inaction" and challenged those that had invested in biosecurity to deploy their resources to stem the epidemic (MSF 2014c, 2014f).

Who, after all, was in charge? This core concern of security thinking grew increasingly unclear in the absence of effective national health care (Abramowitz 2014). Although WHO had global authority, its mission historically emphasized policy rather than direct action; even the Epidemic and Pandemic Alert and Response Program promised "support" to member states in the African region rather than overt leadership (WHO 2014).[6] The CDC ultimately remained an arm of another national

---

4 Hewlett and Hewlett (2008:44) suggest that a survivor or elder would care for the afflicted.

5 For a timeline of events, see http://www.cnn.com/interactive/2014/11/health/ebola-outbreak-timeline/

6 As noted in several news reports, WHO had also suffered budget cuts (Fink 2014; Sun et al. 2014).

government, however large and influential it might be. For its part, MSF would never claim a coordination role as a nongovernmental organization (NGO), and could not realize it even if they wished (MSF 2014a). Although the group found itself playing a prominent part, treating 3,500 confirmed patients by early November (of whom more than 1,400 survived), this was only about a fifth of even the suspect official numbers.[7] And when a handful of international volunteers themselves became sick, their return home for treatment sparked a resurgence of nationalist concerns about borders and quarantines. While no expense might be spared in seeking to care for these lives (and the mortality rate for those evacuated to well-equipped settings appear much lower), the moral heroes of humanitarian medicine had become a potential threat.[8]

The story of Ebola is a tale of medical vulnerability—vulnerability not simply of patients, or even caregivers, but also of systems, including those that seek preparedness. Lulled by plans and simulations, the reflected glow of efficient logistics, and lives saved elsewhere, the global gaze overlooked the blindness of its own policies and a failure to establish or support infrastructure

---

7　See http://www.msf.org/diseases/ebola and http://www.nytimes.com/interactive/2014/07/31/world/africa/ebola-virus-outbreak-qa.html.

8　See Benton (2014) on the differential national/racial valuation of lives. As of December 2, The New York Times reported 20 cases of Ebola treatment outside of Africa, five of which ended in death (an effective mortality rate of 25%, including examples of last minute care) (see http://www.nytimes.com/interactive/2014/07/31/world/africa/ebola-virus-outbreak-qa.html?_r=0)

Ethical Journey of Doctors Without Borders.

BIBLIOGRAPHY

Abramowitz, Sharon Alane. 2014. "How the Liberian Health Sector Became a Vector for Ebola." *Fieldsights–Hot Spots, Cultural Anthropology Online,* October 7. Available at http://www.culanth.org/fieldsights/598-how-the-liberian-health-sector-became-a-vector-for-ebola.

Baert, Bruno. 2001. "Ebola Outbreak Preparedness and Management." November.

Beisel, Uli. 2014. "On Gloves, Rubber and the Spatio-Temporal Logics of Global Health." *Somatosphere,* October 6. Available at http://somatosphere.net/2014/10/rubber-gloves-global-health.html.

Benton, Adia. 2014. "Race and the Immuno-Logics" of Ebola Response in West Africa." *Somatosphere,* September 19. Available at http://somatosphere.net/2014/09/race-and-the-immuno-logics-of-ebola-response-in-west-africa.html.

Caduff, Carlo. 2014. "On the Verge of Death: Visions of Biological Vulnerability." *Annual Review of Anthropology,* 43(8): 1–17.

Centers for Disease Control (CDC). 2014. "Outbreaks Chronology: Ebola Virus Disease." Available at http://www.cdc.gov/vhf/ebola/outbreaks/history/chronology.html.

Christensen, Jen. 2014. "'Out of Control': How the World Reacted as Ebola Spread." *CNN Health.* Available at http://www.cnn.com/interactive/2014/11/health/ebola-outbreak-timeline/.

Cooper, Helene, and Sabrina Tavernise. 2014. "Health Officials Reassess Strategy to Combat Ebola in Liberia." *The New York Times,* November 12. Available at http://www.nytimes.com/2014/11/13/world/africa/officials-consider-scaling-back-of-ebola-centers-in-liberia.html.

Deutsche Welle. 2014. "Germany Unveils Ebola Evacuation Plane in Berlin." November 27. Available at http://www.dw.de/germany-unveils-ebola-evacuation-plane-in-berlin/a-18092535.

Dixon, Robyn. 2014. "Aid Group Has Set the Gold Standard on Ebola Safety." *Los Angeles Times,* October 16. Available at http://www.latimes.com/world/africa/la-fg-ebola-doctors-without-borders-20141016-story.html%23page=1#page=1.

Fink, Sheri. 2014. "Cuts at W.H.O. Hurt Response to Ebola Crisis." *The New York Times,* September 3. Available at http://www.nytimes.com/2014/09/04/world/africa/cuts-at-who-hurt-response-to-ebola-crisis.html?_r=1.

Fox, Renee. 2014. *Doctors Without Borders: Humanitarian Quests, Impossible Dreams of Médecins Sans Frontières.* Baltimore, MD: Johns Hopkins University Press.

Frankfurter, Raphael. 2014. "The Danger of Losing Sight of Ebola Victims' Humanity." *The Atlantic,* August 22. Available at http://www.theatlantic.com/health/archive/2014/08/the-danger-in-losing-sight-of-ebola-victims-humanity/378945/.

Gallagher, James. 2014. "Ebola Test Offering 15-Minute Results on Trial in Guinea." *BBC News,* November 28. Available at http://www.bbc.com/news/health-30243636.

Hewlett, Barry S., and Bonnie L. Hewlett. 2008. *Ebola, Culture, and Politics: The Anthropology of an Emerging Disease.* Belmont, CA: Thomson Wadsworth.

Lachenal, Guillaume. 2014. "Ebola 2014. Chronicle of a Well-Prepared Disaster." *Somatosphere,* October 31. Available at http://somatosphere.net/2014/10/chronicle-of-a-well-prepared-disaster.html.

Lakoff, Andrew. 2014. "Further Reflections on 'Two Regimes of Global Health': On the Elision of Distinctions." *Humanity Journal,* June 9. Available at http://www.humanityjournal.net/blog/further-reflections-on-two-regimes-of-global-health-on-the-elision-of-distinctions/.

McCoy, Terrence. 2014. "Why the Brutal Murder of Several Ebola Workers May Hint at More Violence to Come." *The Washington Post,* September 19. Available at http://www.washingtonpost.com/news/morning-mix/wp/2014/09/19/why-the-brutal-murder-of-eight-ebola-workers-may-hint-at-more-violence-to-come/.

Médecins Sans Frontières (MSF). 2005. "What Kind of Case Management: Patients or Pathologies?" *MSF Messages* 138 (November): 13–14.

———. 2014a. "Ebola: MSF Should Not Replace Governmental Responsibilities." October 31. Available at http://www.msf.org/article/ebola-msf-should-not-replace-governmental-responsibilities.

———. 2014b. "First Trials for Ebola Treatments to Start at MSF

(Beisel 2014). And here perhaps lies a moral: there is no packaged substitute for an effective health care system. When finally galvanized into action, other actors have sought to scale up MSF's approach, building more treatment units along the lines of the group's "gold standard" of care (Wingard 2014; see also Dixon 2014). Even if this tactic ultimately helps contain the outbreak, it only produces a temporary, specialized assemblage rather than a durable network of care (Cooper and Tavernise 2014). In addition to this scaled-up response, and a flurry of efforts to develop treatments and vaccines, the epidemic has also inspired a wave of technical innovation. From a retrofitted German passenger jet to ferry the fortunate few back to gleaming medical centers, to a solar-powered "mobile suitcase laboratory" developed at the Pasteur Institute in Dakar to offer test results in 15 minutes, to an improvised version of personal protective equipment created by a Liberian nursing student, the human capacity for ingenuity has produced an impressive display (*Deutsche Welle* 2014; Gallagher 2014; Park and Umlauf 2014). Yet the mode remains largely piecemeal and reactionary. Similarly, the home disinfection kits MSF began distributing in Liberia, like the clinical trials they have agreed to host, represent a desperate rather than triumphant mode of experiment. When fear and compassion meet, amid terror and chaos, best procedure reveals itself to be "an imperfect solution in a situation that is far from ideal" (MSF 2014e; see also MSF 2014b). It is hard to imagine a more painful illustration of both hubris and limits in global health. ■

PETER REDFIELD *is Professor of Anthropology at University of North Carolina, Chapel Hill and the author of* Life in Crisis: The

Sites in December." November 13. Available at http://www.msf.org/article/first-trials-ebola-treatments-start-msf-sites-december.

———.2014c. "Global Bio-Disaster Response Urgently Needed in Ebola Fight." September 2. Available at http://www.msf.org/article/global-bio-disaster-response-urgently-needed-ebola-fight.

———. 2014d. "Guinea: Mobilisation Against an Unprecedented Ebola Epidemic." March 31. Available at http://www.msf.org/article/guinea-mobilisation-against-unprecedented-ebola-epidemic.

———. 2014e. "Liberia: Distributing Home Disinfection Kits in West Point Suburb." November 5. Available at http://www.msf.org/article/liberia-distributing-home-disinfection-kits-west-point-suburb.

———. 2014f. "MSF International President United Nations Special Briefing on Ebola." September 2. Available at http://www.msf.org/article/msf-international-president-united-nations-special-briefing-ebola.

———. 2014g. "MSF Remains Vigilant as Ebola Outbreak Continues in Guinea and Liberia." May 2. Available at http://www.doctorswithoutborders.org/news-stories/field-news/msf-remains-vigilant-ebola-outbreak-continues-guinea-and-liberia.

———. 2014h. "Sierra Leone: MSF Suspends Emergency Pediatric and Maternal Services in Gondama." Press release, October 16. Available at http://www.doctorswithoutborders.org/article/sierra-leone-msf-suspends-emergency-pediatric-and-maternal-services-gondama.

Médecins Sans Frontières (MSF)–Holland. 2001. "Justice and MSF Operational Choices." Report of discussion held in Soesterberg, Netherlands, June 2001.

Nguyen, Vinh-Kim. 2014. "Ebola: How We Became Unprepared, and What Might Come Next." *Fieldsights–Hot Spots, Cultural Anthropology Online,* October 7. Available at http://www.culanth.org/fieldsights/605-ebola-how-we-became-unprepared-and-what-might-come-next.

Park, Sung-Joon, and René Umlauf. 2014. "Caring as Existential Insecurity: Quarantine, Care, and Human Insecurity in the Ebola Crisis." *Somatosphere,* November 24. Available at http://somatosphere.net/2014/11/caring-as-existential-insecurity.html.

Redfield, Peter. 2013. *Life in Crisis: The Ethical Journey of Doctors Without Borders.* Berkeley: University of California Press.

Sáez, Almudena, Ann Kelly, and Hannah Brown. 2014. "Notes from Case Zero: Anthropology in the Time of Ebola." *Somatosphere,* September 16. Available at http://somatosphere.net/2014/09/notes-from-case-zero-anthropology-in-the-time-of-ebola.html.

Sterk, Esther. 2008. "Filovirus Haemorrhagic Fever Guideline" Médecins Sans Frontières. Available at http://www.medbox.org/ebola-guidelines/filovirus-haemorrhagic-fever-guideline/preview?q=.

Sun, Lena H., Brady Dennis, Lenny Bernstein, and Joel Achenbach. 2014. "How Ebola Sped Out of Control." *The Washington Post,* October 4. Available at http://www.washingtonpost.com/sf/national/2014/10/04/how-ebola-sped-out-of-control/.

Wald, Priscilla. 2008. *Contagious: Cultures, Carriers, and the Outbreak Narrative.* Durham, NC: Duke University Press.

Wieners, Brad, and Makiko Kitamura. 2014. "Ebola: Doctors Without Borders Shows How To Manage a Plague." *BloombergBusinessWeek,* November 13. Available at http://www.businessweek.com/articles/2014-11-13/ebola-doctors-without-borders-shows-how-to-manage-a-plague.

Wilson, Jacque. 2014. "8 Killed in Guinea Town over Ebola Fears." *CNN Health,* September 19. Available at http://www.cnn.com/2014/09/19/health/ebola-guinea-killing/.

World Health Organization (WHO). 2014. "Epic and Pandemic Alert and Response." *WHO Regional Office for Africa.* Available at http://www.afro.who.int/en/clusters-a-programmes/dpc/epidemic-a-pandemic-alert-and-response.html.

Wingard, Morgana. 2014. "Andrew Hill: 'There's No Standard Blueprint for an Ebola Treatment Unit.'" *USAID,* October 1. Available at http://blog.usaid.gov/2014/10/andrew-hill-theres-no-standard-blueprint-for-an-ebola-treatment-unit/.

GLOBAL HEALTH DOESN'T EXIST

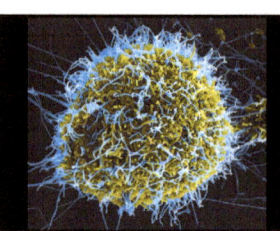

Global health is like the viruses it claims to be combatting; Theresa MacPhail **explains how.**

IF THERE'S ONE THING that the continuing Ebola outbreak in West Africa should have taught us by now, it's this: global public health doesn't exist.

At least not in any type of substantial, material way that might have made our collective response to this devastating epidemic more effective at a far earlier stage in its development. Global health is more concept than concrete reality. What we think of as "global health" is an idea or an organizational model for an integrated international network of health professionals capable of responding to an outbreak of infectious disease anywhere, anytime. But as it currently exists, or at least as it is defined by the various institutions that embrace that label for their projects—a long list that includes everyone from the U.S. Agency for International Development (USAID) to Médecins Sans Frontières (MSF; Doctors Without Borders)—global health remains more aspiration than actuality.

In the current Ebola crisis, the World Health Organization (WHO) is the symbolic figurehead of the global public health network. As such, it carried the brunt of the blame for the slow-paced international response to the outbreaks in West Africa. Initial cases in late March garnered a speedy response, with a whole host of international experts descending on the scene in Guinea and Liberia (including an large team from the U.S. Centers for Disease Control [CDC] Epidemiological Intelligence Service). But, experts argued, the international response did not adequately escalate in proportion to the threat the Ebola virus posed as the situation worsened. It took months for the WHO to issue a public health emergency of international concern (PHEIC), a crucial action in terms of gathering the necessary increased resources, funding, and staff needed to combat the virus effectively. In this sense, "global" health seemed to fail in one of its key tasks.

The WHO, in many ways, is global health. The WHO exists to organize international resources, to be an information hub for all signatory members, to keep tabs on chronic and infectious diseases affecting health everywhere, and to alert member nations when a local outbreak threatens to spread internationally. It also sets international health standards, requires member nations to have actionable epidemic response plans, and advocates for health as a basic human right. As part of this mission, it rallies member nations around central goals for development and disease eradication. As a global institution, the WHO's fundamental mission is to promote health and equal access to health care no matter where individuals are located on the world map. But as an entity whose duty it is to stand vigilant against the spread of infectious diseases around the globe, the WHO is not even half as big as it would need to be to do the job on its own. It simply doesn't have the materials to do so.

Global public health is much like a virus. Like the viruses it helps to eradicate and control, global health cannot survive outside of a healthy "host." The global health network requires the existence of effective local and national public health agencies to function at all. And this "global" network only pulses into material being during large-scale, widespread events such as an influenza pandemic or the current Ebola crisis. The remainder of the time, during more routine outbreaks, it exists in a state of perpetual readiness and watchfulness. Most of the time, the global health network is in a dormant state.

In other words, global health is as viral as the microbes it is called on to battle. ■

THERESA MACPHAIL *is an Assistant Professor at Stevens Institute of Technology and the author of* The Viral Network: A Pathography of the H1N1 Influenza Pandemic.

VIRUS	GLOBAL HEALTH
Needs a host cell	Needs a host institution
Cannot function alone	Cannot function without the local
Mutates to survive	Mutates to expand
Swaps info (gene segments) inside host	Shares info (expertise) inside hosts

Ebola, chimeras, and unexpected speculation

Alex Nading explains how brincidofovir's path to the front lines of the Ebola crisis underscores the contingent, speculative, "chimeric" nature of contemporary global health.

IF YOU WERE STUDYING EBOLA before 2014, chances are that you wouldn't have heard of brincidofovir, an antiviral drug created by a North Carolina company called Chimerix. Within the span of a few weeks in October and November 2014, however, brincidofovir became one of the most promising Ebola countermeasures in clinical development. The story of the drug's path to the front lines of the Ebola crisis underscores the contingent, speculative, "chimeric" nature of contemporary global health.

BRINCIDOFOVIR WAS NEVER MEANT to be an Ebola drug. It was designed, in part, as a smallpox therapy. Commercial drug makers have had vaccines and drugs for smallpox and Ebola in their pipelines for some time, but the market has tended to be too small to attract much private investment. Although humanitarian groups have publicly encouraged (and financially pushed) pharmaceutical companies to develop treatments for "neglected diseases," until very recently, they gave Ebola minimal attention in these efforts (McGoey et al. 2001).

In fact, U.S. biopreparedness programs were paying more attention to Ebola, which joined smallpox on a list of "select agents." In the wake of a series of international bioterror attacks in the 1990s, the U.S. Department of Defense (DOD) began investing in pharmaceutical countermeasures to potential bioterror threats, including anthrax, smallpox, and Ebola. After the 2001 anthrax scare, the National Institute for Allergy and Infectious Diseases (NIAID)—a domestic agency of the Department of Health and Human Services (HHS)—saw an increase in its budget for biothreat research. Both DOD and NIAID used this money to entice private pharmaceutical companies to develop drugs and vaccines, but by the end of the George W. Bush administration, billions in (largely uncoordinated) military and civilian investments failed to move most potential countermeasures out of the laboratory and into late-stage clinical trials. This became painfully clear in 2014 when supplies of ZMapp, a drug that showed potential against Ebola in early animal studies, quickly ran out. Even though HHS had founded the Biomedical Advanced Research and Development Authority (BARDA) in 2006 to move drugs like ZMapp from labs to clinical development more efficiently, the agency's funding had consistently fallen short of the totals necessary for full-scale tests (Greeley and Chen 2014).

Amid this series of bureaucratic and appropriations missteps, the government did have a few successes. Brincidofovir was one of them. It was just the kind of drug that the government's medical countermeasure programs were initiated to support, a therapy that would be effective in patients already infected with a virus: the *smallpox* virus. Chimerix received millions in funding, first from the NIAID and later from BARDA. The company fought vigorously for BARDA's attention, even filing a complaint with the U.S. Government Accountability Office (GAO) in 2011 when BARDA inserted an option into its contract with a competitor firm to purchase millions of extra doses of its prospective smallpox therapy. The GAO upheld Chimerix's complaint. The company used the language of biopreparedness and market fairness to justify the complaint, saying that the GAO's decision to nullify BARDA's option to buy extra doses of the competing product "allows BARDA the opportunity to competitively procure a second smallpox antiviral, consistent with the U.S. government's long-stated strategy of having two smallpox antiviral drugs for protecting the public against the intentional or unintentional release of the smallpox virus" (Chimerix 2011).

BRINCIDOFOVIR IS A "PRODRUG," a weakened form of the antiviral cidofovir. It becomes fully active only when human

Chimerix rings the bell at NASDAQ.

of $14 per share to $35 per share, and the company raised more than $121 million in a stock offering (Chimerix 2014a).

Chimerix's approach to Ebola trials for brincidofovir was initially *domestic* and *defensive*. As the company's chief medical officer explained when the trials were announced, "Our objective is really for us to determine what the safety and antiviral activity is of brincidofovir when used to treat Ebola virus, and *really in the setting of the U.S.*, where we have patients that are basically being relocated from the West African theater, or in patients…who

used in a clinical Ebola trial in West Africa, operated with the support of Oxford University and the Oxford-based International Severe Acute Respiratory and Emerging Infection Consortium (ISARIC) (Chimerix 2014b). ISARIC, an initiative to facilitate open-access protocols and data sharing in clinical research on acute respiratory diseases including SARS, bird flu, and swine flu, is partnering with Médecins Sans Frontieres (MSF; Doctors Without Borders), a humanitarian organization that has been confronting Ebola outbreaks for decades, to help design and plan the trial. ISARIC's pivot from its focus on respiratory diseases like SARS to viral hemorrhagic fevers like Ebola was propelled by a WHO initiative and a 3.2-million-pound grant from the Wellcome Trust (Wellcome Trust 2014). Less than a week later, the Bill and Melinda Gates Foundation committed $5.7 million to a similar multidrug trial in Africa, also including brincidofovir (Bracken 2014). Brincidofovir's prodrug design made it highly portable and suitable for oral ad-

---

At no point did BARDA couch smallpox (or anthrax or Ebola) as a matter of humanitarian concern.

---

bodies begin to metabolize it. This makes it potentially more suitable in patients already infected with smallpox and other DNA viruses. Until recently, no one had considered brincidofovir's efficacy in patients infected with RNA viruses like Ebola. In early 2014, however, Chimerix was asked to provide brincidofovir to the U.S. Centers for Disease Control (CDC) and the National Institutes of Health (NIH) to determine its efficacy against Ebola. Somewhat surprisingly, it showed high potency against the RNA virus in culture (Kroll 2014b). In October 2014, with the ZMapp failure making headlines and other therapies such as Tekmira's TKM-Ebola causing worry about harsh side effects, Chimerix received U.S. Food and Drug Administration (FDA) approval to test brincidofovir in U.S. patients with Ebola (Racaniello 2014). One of the first recipients was Thomas Eric Duncan, the Liberian man who remains the only person to die of Ebola on U.S. soil (Kroll 2014a). At the time of these American tests, one financial analyst noted that Chimerix "shares [were] likely to be (awkwardly) tracking the fate of the Ebola outbreak" (Tirrell 2014). Indeed, by November, the company's stock rose from a midyear low

presented with Ebola virus disease in the U.S." (Loftus 2014; emphasis added). The use of the military term "theater" here is telling. BARDA's interest in smallpox (for which brincidofovir was to be a countermeasure) stemmed in part from a wartime mindset: in the early 2000s, smallpox attack scenarios were at the heart of a civilian-cum-military biopreparedness complex (Lakoff 2008). While a "natural" disease outbreak such as the 2014 Ebola event was one of the many scenarios for which planners had prepared, at no point did BARDA couch smallpox (or anthrax or Ebola) as a matter of *humanitarian* concern. Rather, it was framed as a threat to U.S. lives and property. Testing it in the context of a medical infrastructure that had been preparing for more than a decade to address a novel biothreat from a neglected pathogen seemed most appropriate. Chimerix claimed it needed that infrastructure to carry out its trial, and its public communications expressed uncertainty about "whether brincidofovir is effective in the West African theater" (Loftus 2014).

Just one month later, however, on November 13, Chimerix announced that brincidofovir would be one of two drugs

ministration. In addition, the drug's history of human clinical trial success (albeit in trials against DNA viruses) made it a good bet (Kroll 2014b).

Chimerix, a pharmaceutical firm once seeded by BARDA to build countermeasures against domestic biothreats, was now joining the world's most prominent humanitarian medical institutions: MSF and the Gates Foundation. Thus, brincidofovir has drifted from one pharmaceutical infrastructure to another: it has been partially disembedded from the biopreparedness complex in which it was incubated, and moved to the humanitarian complex where it provides hope. The company's leaders now find themselves in novel ethical territory. Chimerix's CEO told attendees at a biotech conference in December 2014 that "innovation [is] not just in the products, but in the trial design." Brincidofovir will not be tested in randomized control trials with placebo, but in adaptive trials that provide treatment to all infected patients (Oleniacz 2014). Meanwhile, MSF is pushing Ebola drugmakers, including Chimerix, to scale up production of their drugs in advance of trial completion (Moran 2014).

TRIAL DRUGS FOR TREATMENT OF THE EBOLA VIRUS

TRIALS ON THREE DIFFERENT EBOLA TREATMENTS WILL BEGIN IN WEST AFRICA IN DECEMBER, INCLUDING TWO ANTI-VIRAL DRUGS, CHOSEN DUE TO PROMISING DATA & NON-PROHIBITIVE COSTS. FOR ETHICAL REASONS, NO CONTROL GROUP WILL BE USED IN TRIALS, AND THEY WILL END AHEAD OF SCHEDULE IF IMPROVEMENT TO 40% MORTALITY IS OBSERVED.

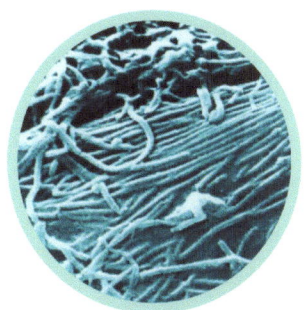

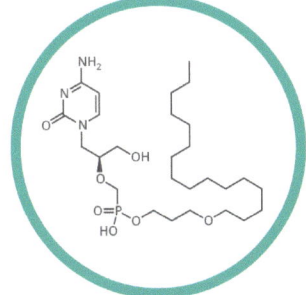

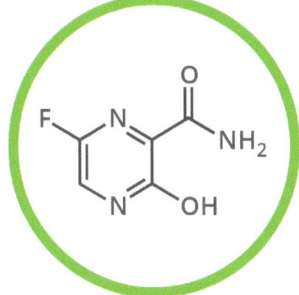

The Ebola Virus

70% WEST AFRICAN DEATH RATE

5000+ DEATHS SINCE OUTBREAK

Effects of the Virus

NAUSEA VOMITING DIARRHOEA RED EYES RASH CHEST PAINS STOMACH PAINS SEVERE WEIGHT LOSS BLEEDING & BRUISING LOSS OF BLOOD FROM ORIFICES DEATH

Brincidofovir

Anti-viral originally developed to treat smallpox, adenovirus, and cytomegalovirus.

Tests on cells in a lab have suggested Brincidofovir could help treat ebola virus.

The first US patient given it at a late stage died, but another patient was subsequently passed ebola-free.

Mechanism unclear - not usually effective against RNA-based viruses like ebola.

Safety tested in 1000+ human subjects. In phase III clinical trials for other viruses in US.

Favipiravir

Anti-viral, active against a range of RNA viruses including influenza & yellow fever.

Appears effective in a mouse model of the ebola virus.

Reported that its administration aided the recovery of a French nurse in Liberia, but its efficacy in human cases is still unclear.

Works by blocking replication of the virus by inhibiting an enzyme.

Already in phase III clinical trials in the US for flu virus treatment.

THIS UNEXPECTED INSTITUTIONAL recombination contains a few lessons for critical scholars of global health. A clue lies in the proto-mythological company name, "Chimerix." The root word "chimera" can connote something spectral or elusive. For many years, the spread of Ebola beyond isolated "hot zones" in Africa's interior was thought to be unlikely without a significant genetic mutation (Preston 1994). In the United States, stories of Ebola epidemics in such zones enabled speculation about whether a mutant strain might wreak havoc on political and economic stability, but most actual epidemics seemed manageable using response kits devised by MSF. As Peter Redfield notes in this issue of *Limn*, MSF's kits helped contain outbreaks, but they could do little to stem the progression of Ebola in infected patients. BARDA was established to develop countermeasures in the event Ebola or another pathogen started to spread at a larger scale, whether through a terror attack or through a "natural" mutation. In addition, a variety of American funders—from USAID to DOD to Google—have begun to support "virus-hunting" projects to identify new pathogens before they emerge. In 2014, the Ebola-related deaths of thousands of West Africans (far outside the original central African "hot zone") revealed that the "global" reach of this predictive biosecurity infrastructure was itself somewhat spectral and elusive. Ebola mutates frequently, but there is no clear evidence that a mutation caused the current crisis. It seems just as likely that transformations in the West African landscape (including deforestation and road building) have combined with increased human mobility and a chronic deficiency in public health infrastructure to make human-to-human transmission possible (Nguyen 2014; Street 2014).

The word "chimera" also refers to a multiheaded monster. Responses to global health crises tend to be governed by what Andrew Lakoff (2010) has called "two regimes," that of humanitarianism and biosecurity. These operations are sometimes enabled (and sometimes hampered) by a third regime: pharmaceutical capitalism. The efforts of the DOD, NIAID, and BARDA to seed the work of companies such as Chimerix (efforts supplemented by the Wellcome Trust and Gates Foundation in the latest Ebola crisis) are one example. Larger corporations like GlaxoSmithKline and Johnson & Johnson, who have had Ebola vaccines in their pipelines for years, have also benefitted from a resurgence of philanthropic, investor, and government support (*The Economist* 2014).

What the story of brincidofovir reveals is that the institutional assemblages of global health operate as much in contingency and chance as in planning and preparedness. The story of the drug's journey from prospective domestic smallpox countermeasure to the front lines of the African Ebola crisis is less one of concerted corporate "rollout" than of recursive scenes of threat and response, sudden promise and enthusiastic investment. Chimeras—monstrous, hybrid, or simply fantastical—tend to be figures of liminality. Their importance is heightened in moments when someone or something sits betwixt and between social categories and states of being (Turner 1964). Drugs like brincidofovir appear promising, but are still short of assured. Likewise, Ebola's shift from potential domestic biothreat to global humanitarian concern is far from complete. If the crisis abates, or if media and lawmakers become crisis-weary, we may see Ebola's profile shift again, from humanitarian concern back to biothreat (and, as the financial pages remind us, Chimerix's stock price may suffer as a result). This uncertainty illustrates the chimeric nature of global health, a network of sites and practices in which crisis is how we come to know life, and how life becomes capital. ▪

ALEX NADING *is Lecturer in Social Anthropology at the University of Edinburgh and author of* Mosquito Trails: Ecology, Health, and the Politics of Entanglement.

BIBLIOGRAPHY

Bracken, David. 2014. "Gates Foundation to Fund Chimerix Drug Trial on Ebola Patients in Africa." *News Observer,* November 19. Available at http://www.newsobserver.com/2014/11/19/4335255_gates-foundation-to-fund-chimerix.html?rh=1.

Chimerix. 2011. "Chimerix and BARDA Reach Agreement Ending GAO Review of Smallpox Antiviral Contract." Press release, June 27. Available at http://ir.chimerix.com/releasedetail.cfm?releaseid=752171.

———. 2014a. "Chimerix Announces Completion of Public Offering of Common Stock and Exercise in Full of Option to Purchase Additional Shares of Common Stock." Press release, November 5. Available at http://ir.chimerix.com/releasedetail.cfm?ReleaseID=880800.

———. 2014b. "Chimerix's Brincidofovir Selected for Use in Ebola Clinical Trial in West Africa by International Consortium." Press release, November 13. Available at http://ir.chimerix.com/releasedetail.cfm?releaseid=882888.

The Economist. 2014. "Giving It a Shot: Drugmakers Bet that Vaccines Will Help in the Fight Against Ebola." November 1. Available at http://www.economist.com/news/business/21629399-drugmakers-bet-vaccines-will-help-fight-against-ebola-giving-it-shot.

Greeley, Brendan, and Caroline Chen. 2014. "How the U.S. Screwed Up in the Fight Against Ebola." *BloombergBusinessweek,* September 24. Available at http://www.businessweek.com/articles/2014-09-24/ebola-drug-zmapps-development-delayed-by-pentagon-agency.

Kroll, David. 2014a. "Chimerix's Brincidofovir Given To Dallas, Nebraska Ebola Patients." *Forbes,* October 7. Available at http://www.forbes.com/sites/davidkroll/2014/10/07/chimerixs-brincidofovir-given-to-dallas-nebraska-ebola-patients/.

———. 2014b. "The Rationale For Clinical Trials of Brincidofovir (BCV) In West African Ebola Patients." *Forbes,* November 13. Available at http://www.forbes.com/sites/davidkroll/2014/11/13/the-rationale-for-using-brincidofovir-bcv-in-ebola-patients/.

Lakoff, Andrew. 2008. "The Generic Biothreat, or, How We Became Unprepared." *Cultural Anthropology,* 23(3):399–428.

———. 2010. "Two Regimes of Global Health." *Humanity,* 1(1):59–79.

Loftus, Peter. 2014. "Chimerix to Conduct Ebola Drug Trial: Drug Company Gets FDA Approval to Start Trial Immediately in Infected Patients." *Wall Street Journal,* October 16. Available at http://www.sanderling.com/Chimerix_%20to_Conduct_Ebola_Drug_Trial.pdf.

McGoey, Lindsay, Julian Reiss, and Ayo Wahlberg. 2011. "The Global Health Complex." *BioSocieties,* 6:1–9.

Moran, Nuala. 2014. "Chimerix, Toyama Drugs, Whole Blood and Plasma in First Ebola Clinical Trials." *BioWorld.* Available at http://www.bioworld.com/content/chimerix-toyama-drugs-whole-blood-and-plasma-first-ebola-clinical-trials-0.

Nguyen, Vinh-Kim. 2014. "Ebola: How We Became Unprepared, and What Might Come Next." *Field Sites-Hot Spots, Cultural Anthropology Online,* October 7. Available at http://www.culanth.org/fieldsights/605-ebola-how-we-became-unprepared-and-what-might-come-next.

Oleniacz, Laura. 2014. "Chimerix CEO Talks about Ethical Challenges of West Africa Ebola Drug Tests." *The Herald Sun,* December 12. Available at http://www.heraldsun.com/news/showcase/x761898222/Chimerix-CEO-talks-about-ethical-challenges-of-West-Africa-Ebola-drug-tests.

Preston, Richard. 1994. *The Hot Zone.* New York: Random House.

Racaniello, Vincent. 2014. "Treatment of Ebola virus infection with brincidofovir." *Virology Blog,* October 9. Available at http://www.virology.ws/2014/10/09/treatment-of-ebola-virus-infection-with-brincidofovir/.

Street, Alice. 2014. "Rethinking Infrastructures for Global Health: A View from West Africa and Papua New Guinea." *Somatosphere,* December 11. Available at http://somatosphere.net/2014/12/rethinking-infrastructures.html.

Tirrell, Meg. 2014. "A Tale of Two Ebola Stocks: Chimerix and Tekmira." *CNBC,* October 9. Available at http://www.forbes.com/sites/davidkroll/2014/10/07/chimerixs-brincidofovir-given-to-dallas-nebraska-ebola-patients/.

Turner, Victor. 1964. "Betwixt and Between: The Liminal Period in Rites of Passage." *Proceedings of the American Ethnological Society,* 4–20.

Wellcome Trust. 2014. "Ebola treatment trials to be fast-tracked in West Africa." Press release, September 23. Available at http://www.wellcome.ac.uk/News/Media-office/Press-releases/2014/WTP057419.htm.

A PHOTO ESSAY

FIGURE 1. Pool of the Palm Camayenne, Conakry. PHOTO: DAOUDA CISSOKO

Frédéric Le Marcis and Vinh-Kim Nguyen document Ebola's ecologies in photos.

YALTA IN WEST AFRICA

Ebola's presence is felt almost immediately upon landing in Conakry. On the way into the city from the airport, judiciously placed billboards dot the landscape, proudly affirming the Guinean government's engagement in fighting the epidemic. In Conakry, as throughout West Africa, buckets of chlorinated water—or sometimes an alcohol-water solution—stand guard, their presence a constant injunction to disinfect one's hands.

The exception to the rule is the Palm Camayenne hotel, located on Conakry's *cornice* (Figures 1, 2). Here, there is no injunction to disinfection: guests can enter unhindered. The Palm Camayenne is one of the rare hotels in Conakry that offers western-style accommodations and 24 hours of electricity and Internet a day. As a result, it has become the home base for the delegations that have been marshalled in the response to the epidemic. Staff from the U.S. Centers for Disease Control (CDC), France's medical research agency INSERM (Institut National de la Santé et de la Recherche Médicale), the Belgian Institute for Tropical Medicine, UNICEF, the World Health Organization (WHO), and many other global health agencies headquarter at the hotel. Ebola is the chief subject of discussion at the Palm Camayenne: the latest government measures, news from the myriad coordination meetings held during the day, epidemiological updates, or the preparation of clinical trials pepper conversations, whether over dinner, at the bar, or poolside.

The hotel even offers a special that includes room and board. Initially called the "Ebola pack," the offer has since been rebranded the "NGO pack": the initial appellation was perhaps subject to misinterpretation. The hotel takes pains to detail the security measures "both active and passive" to ensure against the epidemic, including "hazard analysis critical control point," or HACCP, to ensure food hygiene, constituting a de facto microbiological bunker from which operations can be directed at minimal risk to foreign teams. Ebola too has its Yalta.

FIGURE 2. Courtyard of the Palm Camayenne, Conakry. PHOTO: DAOUDA CISSOKO.

THE BAGHDAD BOYS

In Guinea, as in elsewhere in Africa, youth gangs have become important political actors. Since the end of the régime of Lassana Conté, during the coup that brought the military junta to power, and during the recent elections, Guinean youth groups— going by the English appellation of *Staff*, or *Gang*, or in French, *bande*—have been at the forefront of popular discontent. Despite their association with violence and illicit activities, the youth gangs are nonetheless considered legitimate in their protest against predatory and extractive—in the case of Guinea's mineral wealth—practices. When actors such as

FIGURE 3. PHOTO: DAOUDA CISSOKO

Médecins Sans Frontières (MSF; Doctors Without Borders) or the Red Cross intern patients in camps, "disappear" the bodies of the dead without families present, or bury them in unmarked graves, a powerful symbolic equivalence is established with state predation. It is perhaps not surprising that it is the youth gangs that have instigated at times violent resistance to Ebola efforts: not as a nihilistic gesture, but as a broader politics of rejection of the pillaging of the country by corrupt local and foreign elites.

As central actors of political life in Guinea, youth participate in preventive interventions: in Guéckédou (see Figures 4,5), the "Bagdad staff" organized an Ebola football competition. Whether to contest MSF actions or to foster prevention, youth occupy a place where authorities (elders, the state) are seen as illegitimate. It also signals the subterranean and chronic conflicts that pit generations against each other in a time of diminishing returns.

Ebola crystallizes pre-existing political tensions: between urban elites and rural populations, between elders and youth. Are those in charge of the epidemic there to protect, or just to pilfer the ostentatious display of resources mobilized against the epidemic?

This breakdown in trust, already endemic, has been dramatically heightened with Ebola: the media overload of images of foreign workers in isolation suits, sometimes chasing down escaped patients, saturates questions of social relations and intimacy with the fear of contagion. This epidemic is certainly a political crisis, but it is also a moral crisis.

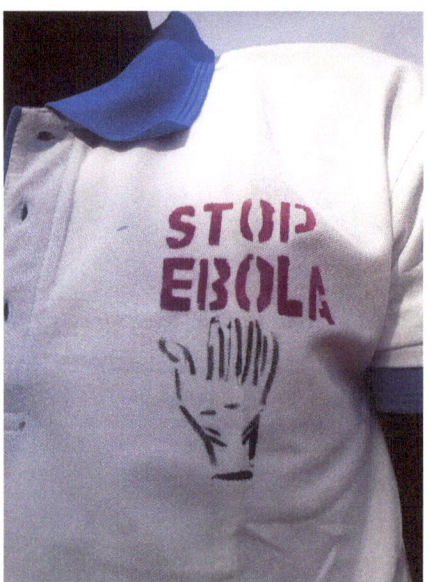

FIGURE 4. Baghdad Staff to Stop Ebola.
PHOTO: F. LE MARCIS.

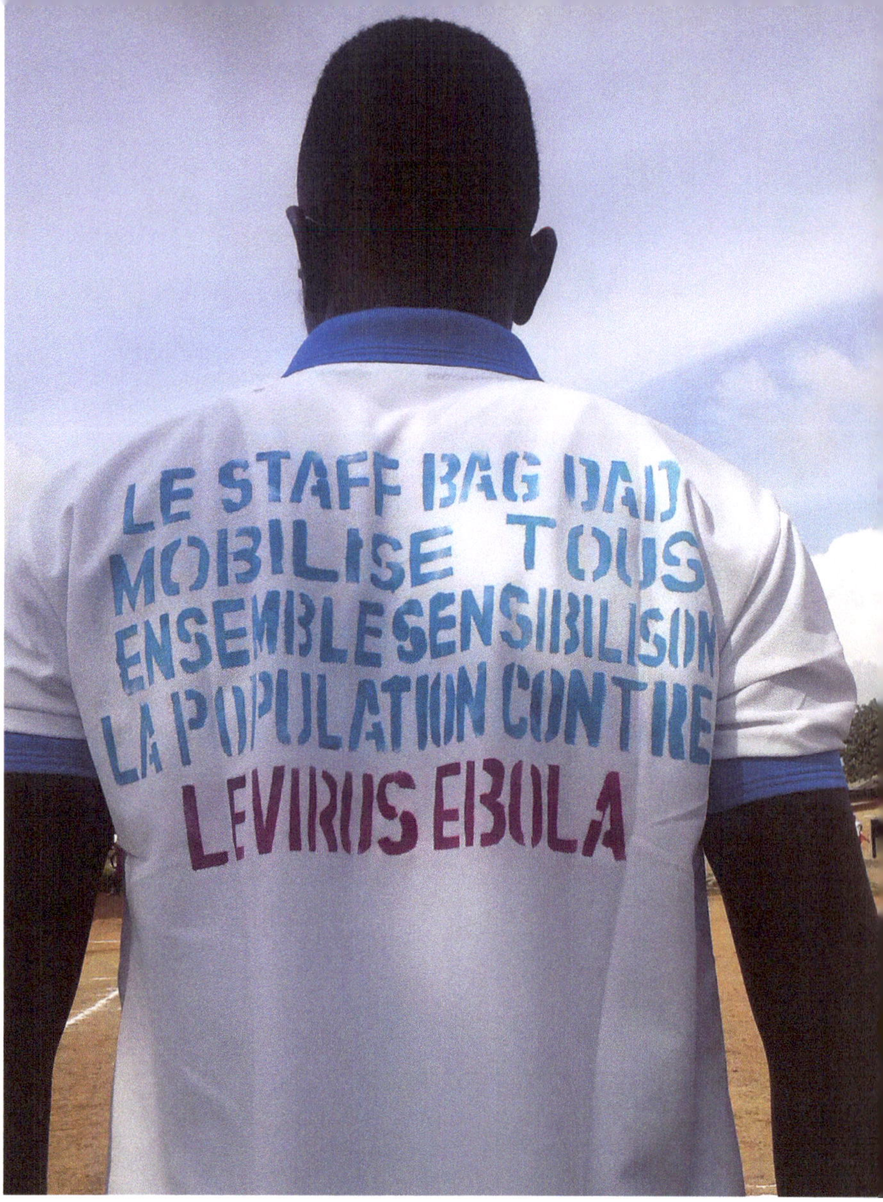

FIGURE 5. PHOTO: F. LE MARCIS.

ON PREPAREDNESS:
GUINEA AS LABORATORY

The Ebola outbreak has put Guinea on the global health map. The engagement of diverse actors aiming at curing or finding proper treatment using gold standard biomedical knowledge production fosters both hope and competition between local actors.

Locals with medical or scientific training have seen the opportunity. One of them (I call him Abdul) takes me to visit his newly opened organization, which surfs on global health key words (*sustainability*, *development*, *health*). In fact, he wants to sell me a product: he is developing a clinic with a lab for running blood tests, and he wants to perform community health surveys. His project seems at first glance dubious, but when we get to his home, things become interesting. He has in fact transformed his domicile, in a well-heeled suburb of Conakry, into a laboratory. We visit the four floors of his house, which is something out of a survivalist manual. The house is off the grid, generating its own electricity with solar panels (with a generator and batteries for back-up) and is self-sufficient in water (well and tanks on the roof). There are a guest apartment, offices, a small canteen also on the roof, classrooms, a conference

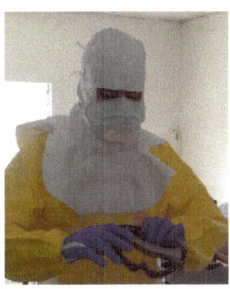

FIGURE 6.
The anthropologist
(FLM) prepares for
fieldwork in an ETU.
PHOTO: DAOUDA CISSOKO.

FIGURE 7. Boarding for Paris, Conakry Airport.
PHOTO: F. LE MARCIS

room with touchscreen, and a fully-equipped P2 lab easily turned into a P3: centrifuges, freezers, PCR booths, etc.

I (FLM) discussed the epidemic with Abdul. He doesn't like the term "postcolonial," although he concedes that one has to understand the "political influences." I ask him why there is not yet a vaccine trial in Guinea. He retorts that France is not "doing its job" even though Guinea is its responsibility: the proof is that at a WHO vaccine meeting at the end of October, the United Kingdom and the United States sent their health ministers, whereas the French "only" sent their Ebola czar. It

has become a common complaint that there is a kind of postcolonial struggle for Africa occurring because of Ebola, with the Americans setting up camp in Liberia, the British in Sierra Leone, and the French in Guinea. Abdul's complaint is different: there needs to be *more* of a scramble and, in a knowing historical analysis, that postcolonial strings are the ones that need to be pulled for this to happen.

FIGURE 8. Ebola preparedness drill in the Emergency Department. PHOTO: V-K NGUYEN.

same time that Thomas Eric Duncan was sent home with Ebola from Texas Presbyterian Health in Houston. Masks and personal protection gear showed up, and drills were conducted. But this kind of preparedness has an Achilles heel: the assumption that it is actually possible to reliably triage those who are stricken with Ebola from those who are not. Most of the health care workers infected with the virus in Africa were not working in specialized Ebola treatment units: they were exposed in the routine work in emergency departments, hospital wards, and maternity units. Patients with Ebola have the same symptoms as those with malaria, or typhoid, or any number of infectious diseases overwhelmingly prevalent in African health care settings, and common in the north. And it is simply not possible to work in those settings cloaked in the kind of personal protective equipment used in Ebola cases.

So might Parisian hospitals be preparing (Figure 8) for the wrong scenario? The current situation (where suspect cases are triaged to specialized hospitals) has put an enormous strain on the affected hospitals. Even though none of the suspected cases has been in fact confirmed, every case mobilizes staff, time, and resources as patients are transferred out of containment wards, clinical and lab staff suit up, and crisis management teams convene. In West Africa, health officials are paying more attention to the coming tsunami of deaths from malaria, childbirth, and other causes of mortality left untreated. But even on remote "front lines" such as in Paris, preparedness for the wrong epidemic may in fact be a distraction from more pressing and immediate health concerns. ∎

FRÉDÉRIC LE MARCIS *is an anthropologist. Professor at the École Normale Supérieure de Lyon and member of the research Team Triangle (UMR 5206). He has worked in West and Southern Africa on Health issues.* **VINH-KIM NGUYEN** *is a medical anthropologist and physician specializing in Emergency Medicine and Infectious Diseases.*

ON PREPAREDNESS: DRILLS AND ANGST ON REMOTE FRONT LINES

The emergency room where I (VKN) work is another kind of Ebola front line: Hospital A, the first major teaching hospital between Charles de Gaulle Airport and the city of Paris, lies amid a ring of *cités* (projects) that form a beltway of urban poverty around northeastern Paris. The vast majority of patients are migrants, many from West Africa. As a result, many who work there consider Hospital A the "front line" for the first domestic Ebola cases. However, preparedness for Ebola has focused on a larger Parisian hospital and a military hospital in the wealthier southern suburbs where all the expatriates

with Ebola brought back to France have been treated—and cured. Preparedness in France rests on two fundamental assumptions: that Ebola patients can be screened prior to boarding flights to Paris (using pistol-like thermometers to take temperatures before boarding, as shown in Figure 7), and that potential cases that get through will be triaged over the phone by France's unique emergency medicine system *before* they arrive at health care facilities.

At Hospital A, preparations for handling Ebola cases were slow to start, but gradually picked up steam around the